NETWORKING FOR AUTHORS

DALE L. ROBERTS

"*Networking for Authors* is a thoughtful guide not only explaining how to network, but why authors should want to network ... Dale's model follows the example he sets in his day-to-day life: be a great person, connect great people, and help make great things happen."

— Jeanne De Vita, Founder of Book Genie

"There are few people I know who could take a word like "networking" which for many writers, is loaded with anxiety and negative emotions, and leverage it in the same positive way that Dale L. Roberts constantly forges valuable, up-beat, and win-win relationships with colleagues."

— Mark Leslie Lefebvre, Author of *A BOOK IN HAND* & WIDE FOR THE WIN

"Dale's unique approach to networking focuses not on 'what's in it for me' but rather 'what's in it for both of us,' which encourages forming genuine, personal connections rather than transactional ones."

— Matty Dalrymple, The Indy Author, Author of *From Page to Platform: How to Succeed as an Author Speaker*

"Whether you're an introvert or seasoned connector, Dale's proven techniques will show you how to build a strong network, foster long-lasting relationships, and supercharge your writing career."

— April M Cox, Award-Winning Author, YouTuber and Creator of *Self-Publishing Made Simple*

"This is the complete guide you need to build strong bridges, nurture deep connections, and grow your author brand. Dale L. Roberts is an expert connector who will show you the way."

— Hannah Jacobson, Founder of Book Award Pro

"Dale is a networking MASTER. ... *Networking for Authors* breaks down his methods, providing a blueprint for any author to build a supportive and impactful network."

— Shanon "S.D." Huston, Author & YouTuber

"Far beyond a 'how-to' book, Roberts masterfully describes the joy of making meaningful, lasting connections with like-minded people."

— Jim Azevedo, Head of Marketing, Draft2Digital

"Whenever I need to connect with someone in the publishing world, Dale Roberts is my first call. His networking savvy has opened countless doors for me and others, and now you can have his entire playbook in your pocket—an absolute must-have for authors."

— Julie Broad, Founder of Book Launchers

"Dale is one of the best in the world at helping authors navigate the overwhelming world of publishing. ... by following the strategies laid out in this book, I now have a clear action plan for success."

— Justin Moore, Author of *Sponsor Magnet*

"*Networking for Authors* offers invaluable insight into the power of relationships in the writing world. Dale's approach highlights how meaningful relationships can be a game-changer for self-published authors. ... A must-read for anyone looking to grow their self-publishing business!"

— Nuria Corbi, Award-Winning Author & Host of *The Home Boss*

"Dale brings the receipts. He's got tons of personal stories to illustrate how you can take networking beyond mere business transactions. His approach emphasizes genuine relationship-building, turning networking from a chore into an opportunity for friendship."

— Evan Gow, Indie Developer of StoryOrigin

"Roberts's gift for writing and knack for crafting palpable passages is encapsulated in lines like, 'While the rising tide raises all boats, your boat has to be in the same harbor as the others.' There is so much to learn and take away from this book!"

— Steven Seril, Founder & President of Outstanding Creator Awards

"Dale Roberts is literally one of the most splendid surprises in my professional career. He is the synthesis of "blossoming and leaning into it" that all at once amuses, amazes and authenticates what diligence can do."

— Dr. Rod Bailey, Dale's former boss & networking mentor

"Dale's commitment to uplifting and supporting others in their creative journey is on full display in this book; it's an asset to everyone lucky enough to come across it."

— Chelsea Bennett, Education & Community Manager at Lulu

"Dale shares his years of personal experience to effectively illustrate his points and his casual writing style makes this a fun and entertaining read."

— Self Pub with Andy, Author & YouTuber

"Networking isn't just a 'nice-to-have'; it's really about finding those people who get you—people who help turn your dreams into plans and your plans into action. ... You never know when a casual chat will turn into a game-changing opportunity."

— Kathleen Sweeney, COO of Book Brush

"*Networking for Authors* is an absolute must for any writer looking to take their career to the next level. ... Dale's strategies have been a game-changer for me, both professionally and personally."

— Jonny Andrews, Book Marketing Expert & Online Business Strategist

"Among the keenest and kindest people I've met in my two decades in the publishing industry, Dale has an incredible knack for not only connecting with people, but in connecting people with one another. ... he's someone who really cares about seeing others succeed and encourages them along the way."

— Jason Jones, Publicist at Jones Literary

"Dale is a powerhouse in the networking space. His ability to make new connections and link others is unmatched. When it comes to networking, there is no one better to take your networking game to the next level."

— Marco Moutinho, Founder & CEO of Dibbly

Networking for Authors: Strategies to Supercharge Your Writing Career

By Dale L. Roberts
©2024 One Jacked Monkey, LLC

eBook ISBN: 978-1-63925-045-5
Paperback ISBN: 978-1-63925-046-2
Hardcover ISBN: 978-1-63925-047-9
Audiobook ISBN: 978-1-63925-048-6

All rights reserved. No part of this book may be reproduced in any form by any electronic or mechanical means, including information storage and retrieval systems, without permission in writing from the copyright owner, except by a reviewer who may quote brief passages in a review.

Some recommended links in this book are part of affiliate programs. This means if you purchase a product through one of the links, then I get a portion of each sale. It doesn't affect your cost and helps support the cause. If you have any reservations about purchasing a product through my affiliate link, then Google a direct link and bypass the affiliate link.

I dedicate this book to Dr. Rod Bailey, the man who instilled in me the power of networking and building meaningful, long-lasting relationships in all walks of life. I'm forever grateful for the time we spent together.

Win **awards** and get **reviews** for **your book**

25% off your first purchase

bookawardpro.com

"I've used dozens of book cover design services over the last ten years, and none compare to the level of quality and professionalism that Miblart delivers."

— *Dale L. Roberts*

Miblart - a book cover design company for self-published authors

Designers who specialize in different genres	Unlimited number of revisions
No deposit to get started	You can pay in installments

GET A BOOK COVER THAT WILL BECOME YOUR N°1 MARKETING TOOL

Excellent

 4.9

Your Book Marketing Companion

Meet **Dibbly Create.** Your All-in-1 A.I. companion for writing, publishing & marketing your book.

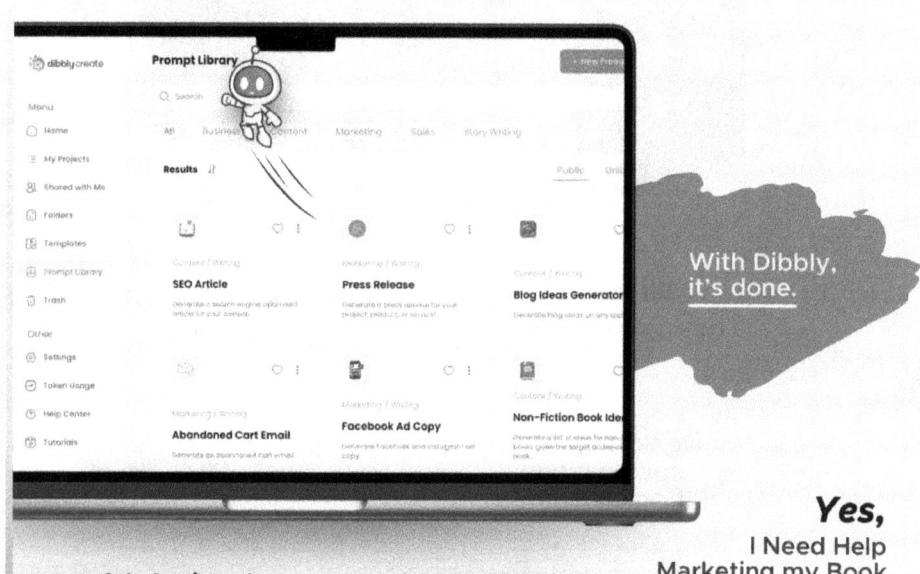

With Dibbly, it's done.

Yes,
I Need Help Marketing my Book

A.I. Assisted:

- ✓ Book descriptions
- ✓ Lead magnet
- ✓ Email copy
- ✓ Subject lines
- ✓ Social media posts
- ✓ Press releases
- ✓ Landing pages
- ✓ Much more

Try for Free!

Scan the QR Code or visit   dibbly.com/create

DRAFT  DIGITAL®

Next level tools to help you grow.

Whether you're an aspiring author or international bestseller, we've got the tools to help you publish faster, distribute wider and manage your business easier.

Learn more by going to **d2d.tips/dale** and read on to discover some of what sets D2D apart:

- ✓ **Automated end-matter**
- ✓ **New Release Notifications for readers**
- ✓ **Payment Splitting for contributors**
- ✓ **Scheduled price changes**
- ✓ **Smashwords store coupons**
- ✓ **Universal Book Links via Books2Read.com**

 **It's print-on-demand reimagined.**

Create a paperback on draft2digital.com from your existing ebook with just a few clicks, and **create a full, wrap-around book cover from your ebook cover**. It really is that easy!

 **THE indie bookstore.**

Massive annual sales, self-serve promotion tools, and the **industry's best royalty rates** of up to 80% list. Readers love discovering breakout indie authors at smashwords.com.

CONTENTS

AN INTRODUCTION TO NETWORKING 1

CHAPTER 1: UNDERSTANDING YOUR NETWORKING GOALS 7

CHAPTER 2: BUILDING AN AUTHOR BRAND 20

CHAPTER 3: OFFLINE NETWORKING STRATEGIES 35

CHAPTER 4: ONLINE NETWORKING STRATEGIES 46

CHAPTER 5: EFFECTIVE COMMUNICATION AND RELATIONSHIP BUILDING 56

CHAPTER 6: LEVERAGING TECHNOLOGY FOR NETWORKING 69

CHAPTER 7: OVERCOMING NETWORKING CHALLENGES. 79

CHAPTER 8: NETWORKING FOR BOOK MARKETING AND PROMOTION 88

CONCLUSION: NETWORKING FOR LONG-TERM SUCCESS 98

A SMALL ASK... 103

ABOUT THE AUTHOR 105

SPECIAL THANKS 106

RESOURCES. 107

AN INTRODUCTION TO NETWORKING

I'm an introvert. Comfort means staying home and doing whatever it takes to avoid actual human interaction. I totally understand that a lot of authors think like I do, so why is it I'm able to consistently connect with other authors and business professionals? What would drive me to meet new people when I have everything I could ever want?

Networking.

It may be a confusing answer for those of you doing the math, but networking is so much more than building and fostering connections. It's truly about locking arms with like-minded, goal-driven maniacs travelling the same path as you.

This adage applies to business *and* life:

Two heads are better than one.

You work at a disadvantage when you work alone. If you're anything like me—an indie author—then chances are you already wear too many hats. By isolating yourself, you're willingly accepting the stress and workload that an entire team oversees at a traditional publishing company.

Imagine if you didn't have to struggle like that anymore. What if you could build a team of folks perfect for your every need?

That's the purpose of building a network.

When thinking about topics for this book, I truly didn't know what I'd write about. I had six nonfiction books simmering on the back burner, ready for release. I felt like my creative well had run dry, and I was completely puzzled about what to do next.

I contacted an old friend, Kathleen Sweeney, from a small graphic design company called Book Brush. Little did I know that she'd provide the inspiration behind this book.

I met Kathleen five years ago when she cold prospected me about her company. Admittedly, I wasn't the least bit interested in what she offered; I get dozens of offers to promote products and services. I usually find products and services I support through research or through word-of-mouth.

There was something different about how Kathleen approached me. It wasn't the same old tired text of:

> *I love your channel. It's my favorite. The episode where you talked about keywords was great. I've got a product you should....*

Pass!

Kathleen's execution was elegant and concise. She may have assumed her email would end up in a slush pile of offers from companies and brands. Yet I still opened her message and read it. I peeked at Book Brush, then politely declined. I couldn't see the difference between using Book Brush and Canva.

I was happy to keep the dialogue going, though, so I asked her to keep me updated on any new features or options.

Within a few months, she pinged me again, this time sharing a new feature they had rolled out. She tapped into something I found interesting, something I could use. Book Brush had a new graphic design option called Instant Mockups which allowed authors to showcase their books using real-life elements (i.e., on bookshelves, in a reader's hand, on the beach). The product doesn't matter in this story as much as the new connection. I fast became a fan of all features within Book Brush and shared it many times with my viewers on YouTube. After that, Kathleen went on to become my biggest supporter and cheerleader.

I didn't invest my interest and trust in the company so much as I did in Kathleen Sweeney. She showed up in a big way first through a professional email. After that, she invested the time to meet me over video chats to see how we could best fit each other's needs.

As the years have passed, I've come to know Kathleen on a deeper level—not just as a peer, but as a friend. So many times when I've needed a little extra help, Kathleen has offered it. For instance, if I publish a book or post a video on YouTube, Kathleen is happy to share them with her audience. Whenever I know another author could benefit from Book Brush, I introduce Kathleen to them.

Sure, I could've easily shared my enthusiasm for Book Brush, but I'm not invested in the company. I'm invested in Kathleen.

Since we've known each other and have communicated regularly over the years, whenever I meet someone who'd benefit from having Kathleen Sweeney in their business network, I make the introduction.

One night, during a casual phone chat with Kathleen, I had a eureka moment. Kathleen never lacks enthusiasm or positivity, so her infectious personality seeped through the phone lines and spilled into my brain in an instant.

Just a few weeks before our call, Kathleen had texted me a picture from the NINC Conference in Florida. In the picture were Kathleen and another friend, M.K. Williams.

I met M.K. years ago when I stumbled upon one of her YouTube videos. Her passion for self-publishing and raw energy attracted me to her content. Naturally, I reached out to her, and a newfound connection and friendship developed. We even collaborated on a video series and had a few masterminds about YouTube with other video creators.

A couple years into knowing M.K., it occurred to me that she needed to meet Kathleen. After all, who wouldn't want to have a positive, uplifting, and energetic personality like Kathleen in their circle?

I also knew M.K.'s audience might appreciate learning about Book Brush. Likewise, Kathleen could have a bona fide YouTube star to share with her current customer base. It was a win for everyone.

In our conversation, Kathleen mentioned getting to meet M.K. in person and how it was quite the experience. It's one thing to meet through video chat, but nothing beats the unseen energy exchange of talking to someone face-to-face.

The picture Kathleen sent touched me on a whole different level. I know this small connection doesn't seem like much. But when I step back and look at the bigger picture, M.K. and Kathleen are more than simply two business professionals connecting; they're conduits for larger communities and opportunities. They wouldn't have received those benefits if they had never met.

Through this one connection, the effects rippled across their communities. When M.K. wants to promote a book, she can lean on Kathleen to help. Or when Book Brush rolls out a new feature, Kathleen can give M.K. a call.

Do they have to oblige every time? No, but it's certainly nice to have someone in your corner from time to time.

How and when you connect two professionals makes a world of a difference. If you blindly start connecting folks without a degree of decorum and delicacy, you might as well flush your entire business network down the drain.

Don't sweat it, though. I'll guide you through some of the unspoken rules of etiquette in networking, discuss what you get from it, and cover how building a deep network of business professionals is the most invaluable asset in your book marketing toolbox.

As you go along, you may find that some suggestions and tips contrast with your nature, and that's fine. Hear me out at least, because I'm an introvert, too. But an introvert who makes some of the biggest networking connections in all of self-publishing.

From small-time YouTubers to major publishing companies.

From aspiring authors to experienced self-publishing experts.

I've built bridges that have opened up my personal success to whole new levels I never imagined. The way I approach networking is with goodwill first, while eventually tending to my needs when it matters.

Hopefully, after this nice shout-out to Kathleen and M.K., they'll promote the heck out of my book. Of course, I say this in jest…

…but at least it's still an option.

In this book, I'll share real examples from my experiences networking. If I use someone's full name, you'll know I'm referring to a real person. When I use first names only, I've changed the names and some identifying details about our relationship to protect the people involved—both the innocent and maybe the guilty.

Now let's explore the wild world of *Networking for Authors,* a guide that'll help even the most seasoned wallflowers to open up and discover a whole new world for building and growing your author brand.

CHAPTER 1
UNDERSTANDING YOUR NETWORKING GOALS

During my time working in the healthcare industry, I had the pleasure of working under a fantastic general manager, Rod Bailey. He had a wealth of experience in all walks of business, having plied his trade in many capacities and roles. He was charming, smart, and quick-witted. Everything about Rod was lovable, and I came to realize fast how much reach and impact he had in his job and community.

Any time Rod headed out of the senior community for events or local meetups, he was quick to take me under his wing and bring me along for the ride. His interaction with other people never disappointed me, both in business and in life. Every time we'd go out, someone inevitably knew Rod. They'd either greet him with a hearty handshake and a clap on the shoulder or, sometimes, a big hug.

Rod seemed ubiquitous around Phoenix, Arizona. I watched him like a hawk, taking mental notes about what he'd do when arriving at a business mixer, how he'd greet other professionals, and what he'd do and say first to break the ice with someone he didn't know. The man was simply fearless. He showed no signs of doubt and exuded confidence in every interaction he had.

Finally, I asked him, "How do so many people know you? And how do you remember them all?"

He laughed and said something like, "It's years of networking and practice."

I'd seen him countless times introduce one professional to another, making himself the perfect hype man. He made me sound like the greatest thing since sliced bread on more than one occasion. Flattery got him everywhere with me. The thing is, he was real and genuine about it. He truly believed in me and my abilities, so he was eager to showcase who I was and why I was the perfect person to connect with.

It didn't even occur to me that the man had taken me under his wing and showed me the art of networking with business professionals. At first sight, it was subtle. Years later, I realized he had mastered the process of meeting, introducing, and connecting people.

His true genius was in leveraging the massive reach within his network to get small favors, make new connections, and elevate his work within the healthcare communities. Whenever he needed a good catering company, he had a contact. Should he need to get donations and contributions to a fundraiser, Rod had the connections. I know that if he ever wanted to attach a flock of balloons to our assisted living community to float off like the house in the movie *Up*, he could do it simply by asking every contact he knew to donate a single balloon.

I never saw Rod sacrifice his integrity or abuse his network just to get ahead of others. He always raised others up around him. That's where the magic happened.

He wasn't just some guy manipulating business professionals in a quid pro quo system; he was a friend who'd have your back in a pinch. Rod was all about making a lasting connection between people while expecting nothing in return.

Let's dissect what Rod did and how you can implement his networking practices so you, too, can have a deep virtual Rolodex of incredible people. When the time comes and you need a little help selling a book, promoting your brand, or elevating your author business, you'll know the perfect person for the job.

Think of your network as a toolbox. Each business professional you've met or gotten to know serves as an invaluable part of your success as an author. If you're new to networking, it's going to take some time to build your list of networking professionals. I'm not saying you need to make a list of everyone you know—that is, unless that's helpful to you.

Before we tackle who you know, what they do, and how you can best serve them, let's define your purpose as an author. You cannot advocate for others without understanding yourself first. When the time is right, you need to share who you are and what you do in a few sentences.

I know that's a stretch for a lot of authors. After all, we're rewarded for being a little extra verbose. When making a first impression, one of the worst things to do is to bloviate endlessly about yourself. I've been to dozens of business meetups and mixers and inevitably there's that one obnoxious person who's busy talking over everyone, stuffing a card into reluctant hands, and being an all-around jack-wagon.

President Theodore Roosevelt once said:

> *Nobody cares how much you know until they know how much you care.*

While it seems counterintuitive to take a backseat to others' needs, it actually works well. I'm not implying that you meet a bunch of people, help them out one time, then expect favors to come raining in all at once. The difference between a good network and a great one is time. You can't expect to build a reliable business network overnight, and I think that's why many folks get discouraged after attempting to network like a boss—or in this case, like Rod.

Rod Bailey was a seasoned pro, having years to practice his chops in networking. The journey of 1,000 miles begins with one step. Lucky for you, all you have to do is turn the page and dig right into it.

DEFINING YOUR OBJECTIVES AS AN AUTHOR

The iconic action film star Arnold Schwarzenegger once said:

> *Who is your daddy and what does he do?*

Part of identifying your objectives starts with knowing who you are and what you bring to a networking relationship. And that means having a succinct way to answer the questions, who are you and what do you do?

The first tip I'd urge you to follow is to craft a simple elevator pitch. Even when you wake from a dead sleep, you need to recite who you are and what you do in a succinct yet compelling way that will capture your audience's attention.

You don't have to go overboard in your delivery or claims. Stick to the facts.

As an example, my elevator pitch is simply:

> *I'm an award-winning author and YouTube video content creator who teaches people how to write and publish books that sell.*

Is it magical or perfect? No, but it gives someone the best overhead view of who I am and what I do. These small morsels are enough for anyone to identify and relate to. After all, who doesn't enjoy reading books, watching YouTube videos, or yearning to write a story that has lived in their heart for ages?

I am constantly refining my elevator pitch as I uncover my strengths and passions. You will develop how to deliver your elevator pitch, too.

Keep in mind, I provided you with the shortest version of my elevator pitch. It's my go-to when meeting with a group of professionals. In a one-on-one scenario, I'll elaborate more if given the time, but I rarely go beyond thirty seconds.

In a lot of first-time conversations, people are sizing you up, getting a read on you, and trying to find some way to relate. If you go on for too long, they're going to tune out and forget most of the things you've said.

Let's craft your elevator pitch now by answering these questions:

1. What is one thing you want to be remembered for *right now*?

2. What *accolades can you share* without sounding like a braggard?
3. What *purpose* do you serve as an author?

While I'd love to write a whole feel-good, self-help segment about believing in what you will be one day, it's not authentic in the present time, nor is that relevant to the person you're just meeting. While you may want to become a bestselling author or a millionaire from your books, if it's not currently true, don't say it to another business professional.

Yes, the Law of Attraction is fine and can work well for some people. Claiming you'll be a millionaire from your books or lying about it is not a favorable impression in a networking situation. You'll get shuffled off to a corner with that obnoxious business card guy. Damn, that guy sucks.

Side note: Never give a business card unless asked or if the conversation leads perfectly into handing one out. I've thrown away some really nice business cards that looked woven by the hand of gods. Why? Because I never wanted it nor had any interest in connecting further with that professional. I may have taken a gorgeous card not because I was interested in the connection, but just because I was afraid of being dragged into another long-winded story about themselves if I didn't. Sheesh, hard pass!

Be real, but also, don't be afraid to find the best way to showcase what you do. You're a freaking author and you have a book or backlist to show for all your hard work. Few people can say they've written, much less published, a book. That's a bigger deal than you know.

Consider the many hats you wear as an author. Most authors are savvy marketers, since we have to promote our books endlessly. Think about other tasks you do to make it all happen, from idea to first draft to editing to formatting to cover design and beyond. Authors have a rather thankless job, especially if you're an indie author.

Looking over those many hats, what are parts of your author business you excel at? Is it writing? Or are you a social media superstar getting tons of engagement from your Instagram posts or TikTok videos? Take nothing for granted when reflecting on the work you've accomplished.

I understand you might not want to brag about what you do, but when you're building a network, it is important to have confidence when sharing what you've accomplished.

The next question on the list allows you to tap into your ability to humble brag. Have you won any awards, gained any recognition for your work, or had anything outstanding happen to you?

You'll notice in my elevator pitch that I simply said I'm an award-winning author. From time to time, I whip out the old "thirty-two-time award-winning author." That's a *huge* flex and will convey with gravity that I've earned the title of author. Do I share those specifics every time? No, because sometimes, it feels a *little* too over the top. Many people would disagree with me on that point, so draw your own conclusion and test what does and doesn't work for you.

I only mention the number of awards when I have that one-on-one experience. In a crowd of people, I keep only the essential need-to-know details in my pitch since most people want time to talk about themselves. Don't worry, you'll still get your time to shine and connect. Just don't make it a huge priority during the first impression.

The last questions are simple, but often authors sell themselves short here. It comes down to why your work serves a greater purpose and who your audience is.

In my pitch, I simply tell folks I teach aspiring authors and established pros how to write and publish books that'll generate more revenue. This brief glance at what I do allows the other person to think about me if they want to explore my area of expertise.

As a published author, you should have already clarified who your audience is and how you serve them; if you haven't, then creating your elevator pitch can be rather difficult. Yes, this applies to fiction too. What you do is just as important as any other niche. I believe Jonny Andrews once proclaimed paranormal romance as books about things that go hump in the night. It's rather cheeky, and may not fit your brand, but as you can tell, his one-liner communicates a little humor while opening up an interesting conversation.

IDENTIFYING YOUR TARGET AUDIENCE & INDUSTRY CONNECTIONS

Think back on any time you've met someone for the first time. It doesn't matter who they were or if they've been part of your life since. Reflect on what crossed your mind as you shook their hand, listened to them speak, and sized them up from top to bottom. You're most likely doing what everyone else does—figuring out how you can relate.

Most folks fall back on small talk, like the weather, sports, or the latest trend online. And while it's not the best first conversation, it certainly serves as a gateway to a more fulfilling dialogue.

I encourage you to take a step back and think of the best way to communicate in a way that expresses your deepest passion and defines the audience you're serving. When someone gets a better idea of your ideal audience—or reader—then they have something to work with beyond how muggy it is in Florida or how freezing it is in Alaska.

I often share an old story that dates back to my time working under Rod Bailey. This networking thing hooked me because it made my job easier. I made it my mission to attend every local Chamber of Commerce meeting. In one of those meetings, I crossed paths with an experienced marketer, Mark Stafford. Our initial introduction was harmless enough since neither of us really had much in common beyond his work in marketing and my work in healthcare.

Fast-forward a year or two later. I had my first published book in hand and was ready to present it to Mark at a local restaurant. I had no intention beyond hooking up my friend with a copy of my crowning achievement. Little did I know, he'd profoundly change my world.

Mark opened my book, thumbed through the pages, and congratulated me on my achievement. Then, he asked a fairly deep question that I initially perceived as rude.

"Who is this book for?" Mark asked.

I didn't even hesitate when I said, "Oh, everyone."

Without even lifting his head, he peered over his glasses at me with a puzzled look.

"Are you telling me you wrote a fitness book for everyone?"

I stammered and struggled to grasp what he was asking and why. Was he telling me my book was garbage? If so, why didn't he just come out and say it? When I couldn't present a reasonable answer, he finally interjected, "Look, Dale, I'm sure this is a great book, but I find it hard to believe you'd give the same fitness advice to a teenager that you'd give a senior citizen. It's just not possible."

He paused, put the book down, and looked directly at me before taking a deep sigh. "When you write for everyone, you write for no one. You absolutely must figure out who your ideal audience is so you write and market a book directly to them. You'll get more sales and grow an audience so much faster than trying to please the masses."

I stewed about that conversation for months after. And the more I thought about it, the more I realized he was right.

In order to truly make an impact as an author with your readers, you've got to get clear on who you're talking to through your books.

Some folks will have you believe you need to have an exact avatar of who your reader is; for the sake of simplicity in this exercise, get at least a general idea of who that is. You don't need to sweat demographics, geography, or any of the granular facts about your audience. After all, can you imagine if I said this:

> *I'm an award-winning author and YouTube video content creator who teaches people between the ages of 25 and 44 heavily skewing male in the United States how to write and publish books that sell.*

That's so oddly specific that you'd get a confused look and a quick end to your introduction. Maybe, just maybe, the deep understanding you have of your audience would impress someone.

When networking, you don't need to get that granular unless someone asks you. And, even then, tread carefully by making sure the other person genuinely cares about that nerd-level data.

Of course, identifying your ideal reader is just as important as knowing your ideal industry connection. I'm not saying you need to dismiss anyone's background or expertise as useless to your needs. But you'll certainly want to invest time and energy in fostering the right long-term relationships.

While not everyone you meet will be a good fit right now, they might be later—if not for you then for someone within your network. Remember this rule when building out your network: Take no one for granted, because that person could be the key ingredient to your breakthrough success.

The most important thing to do when defining your ideal connection is to keep an open mind and when in need—ask. I've found quite a few times when I needed an expert, I could lean on my network to guide me to the right person. You don't have to scour freelance websites and flush money down the toilet when you can get a referral from a reliable peer in your network.

Keeping that person in mind when you need work done or some burning questions answered goes a long way toward them thinking about you when they need an author just like you.

SETTING REALISTIC NETWORKING GOALS

While it's been ten years since I saw Rod Bailey in all his networking glory, some of his indirect lessons in networking remain with me today. Since we already know Rod had years of experience beyond me, we can automatically assume what he did came from years of consistent efforts. He baked networking into his action plan for business, making it essential.

I'm sure he's much like everyone else in that he probably didn't feel like networking or wasn't always at his best, but he at least put in the effort consistently.

Just as you can't expect your book to sell without marketing, your business network won't grow without effort.

Though we'll explore what that means and how to do this, I'll simplify it for right now. Get out and talk to someone, anyone. I don't mean you literally have to leave your house every time to network with folks. We're in a digital age where you're merely a virtual handshake away via video chat on Zoom, Discord, Google Meet, or even an old-fashioned phone call.

The best thing you can do is sit down and write out a list of everyone you know. Look at that list once you run out of names and write up a synopsis of what they do and who they serve. Pinpoint the ones you find most intriguing and why you feel that way about them. Then, pick up the phone, send out an email, and have a conversation with that person, even if it's only for fifteen minutes.

Think about the ways you relate to them and the connections you have that might appreciate this person as well. Most importantly, find out what they need and how you can help them achieve a goal or move forward in their business. Keep in mind, results might not come right away.

This reminds me of conversations I've had with my old friend, Fraysher Ferguson. He was an icon in the world of fitness around Columbus, Ohio—a wellspring of information. Every time I'd visit him, he'd teach me a new exercise. One day I asked him, "How do you know so many exercises? And how can you even remember them all?"

He said the simplest yet most profound statement. "Oh, you'll forget them, but they'll come back to you when you need them most."

While I don't expect you to remember every person's name, occupation, and audience, you will remember some of those folks. You might meet a professional at a library meetup or a book club now, but it might not occur to you how they fit into your overall plan for networking. Until then, don't sweat making every connection work right now. That will come over time with practice, persistence, and a consistent effort.

CHAPTER 2
BUILDING AN AUTHOR BRAND

You never truly get a second chance to make a first impression. Based on your choice to read a book about networking for authors, I'm assuming that you treat your author business seriously. Everything you put out is probably your absolute best effort. After all, no one sets out to be the absolute worst writer on the planet.

Let's consider some of the finer details of building an author brand, especially one that creates the best first impression, leaving an impact on anyone you meet. You want to stand out. After all, the goal of building a deep business network is to help elevate your author brand.

Your author brand includes everything about what you do and who you are. When packaging your brand, account for not just what people read, but what they see, can expect, and can access through you. Let's explore the best first steps.

CRAFTING A COMPELLING AUTHOR BIO

Start with the fundamental element of your author brand identity—a short bio. Many indie authors get this wrong on so many levels because they end up dumping way too much needless and irrelevant info, forcing a potential reader to power through an overstuffed bio that really is a synopsis of their life story.

While no one is going to be in danger of a flogging for a padded or wordy bio, it can certainly create a lot of unnecessary friction for potential readers who want to learn more about you.

Treat business professionals the same way you would a potential reader. You can imagine after someone meets you, they're going to search for your books online and read your bio.

The main point of a bio is to give your readers enough substance to relate to so they understand more about you. When you're crafting that bio, think about the ideal audience you want to attract. Conversely, what you choose will also repel the audience you don't want. This means your bio must be specific, clear, and to the point.

Crafting a bio doesn't require a deep understanding of copywriting, although that doesn't hurt. In the art of copywriting, the point is to get folks to read from top to bottom and take a specific action. While some experts will have you believe a call-to-action is a necessity in your bio, I really think it comes down to preference.

Some authors promote their websites, email newsletters, or latest books. That's fine, but remember, a little goes a long way, so don't give your potential reader too many choices. If they are overwhelmed with options, they may not take any at all. Pick one specific action you want them to take and stick with that.

Crafting your author bio is like creating your elevator pitch. In one to two paragraphs with only 150 to 200 words, describe who you are, what you do, and why you do it.

Many people debate over what works best—first person or third person. It comes down to taste. I prefer third person since it conveys credibility. It's easier for someone else to share I'm a thirty-two-time award-winning author—okay, I swear that's the last flex—and for potential readers to view it as a big deal.

Here's the current iteration of my bio:

Dale L. Roberts is a self-publishing advocate, award-winning author, and video content creator. Dale's inherent passion for life fuels his self-publishing advocacy both in print and online. After publishing over fifty titles and becoming an international bestselling author on Amazon, Dale started his YouTube channel, Self-Publishing with Dale. Selected by Feedspot *and* LA Weekly *as one of the best sources in self-publishing of 2022, Dale cemented his position as the go-to authority in the indie author community.*

Dale currently lives with his wife and two rescue cats in Columbus, Ohio.

I lead with the three most important hats I wear: a proponent of self-publishing, an award-winning author, and a YouTuber.

In the next two sentences, I add more context to those hats I wear, so I clear up any ambiguity. Within those two sentences, I'm clear about what it is I do, who it's for, and how I'm pretty darned good at it.

The last sentence is where some authors would place a call-to-action. I keep it simple. I take pride in my family and the home we've built, so I'll end by introducing them and sharing my homebase. If you aren't comfortable exposing where you live, I totally understand. Anyone wanting to remain anonymous will have a tough time networking, since a lot of it consists of making yourself vulnerable with complete strangers.

Do not be confused; you aren't crafting a great author bio to rattle off at a networking event. This will represent your brand online and in print. Too many authors take this area for granted—which I think is a missed opportunity—while others over-share in their bio. Find the balance in between. Go too short and a reader won't know how they can relate with you. Go too long and only your diehard fans will appreciate the insights.

The rest? Yeah, they tuned out when you went on about all your degrees in college, your hobbies of shuffleboard and pickleball, and your weird attraction to eating Takis in bed. If any of that information bears relevance to the niche you write in, use it. If not, toss it out.

Though I'm a former professional wrestler, I don't have to include that in my bio since my audience comprises writers and self-publishers. Is my wrestling background cool? Sure, but is it relevant? No, it brings nothing of value to the conversation.

Don't be afraid to infuse your personality within the bio and loosely use these rules for crafting your author bio. Once you have an edited second draft of your bio, have a few people proofread it for you—preferably someone who knows you and someone who doesn't know you.

The person who knows you might remind you of something you're missing, like an interesting factoid that could elevate your perceived importance. When someone unfamiliar with you reviews your bio, they're going to attack it from the viewpoint of a potential reader.

It definitely doesn't hurt having more than a couple of people to help. Just don't bog yourself down with too much advice. It's your bio and you have the final say on the final draft.

Remember, you aren't married to this bio, so change it up occasionally, updating facts and info that'll lend more credibility.

When all else fails and you're stumped, consider hiring out or leveraging generative artificial intelligence (A.I.) to write your author bio.

In my video series about building an author brand, I worked with a few freelancers on the Fiverr marketplace—a website that allows customers to order business-related projects. I worked with a few bio writers and found the results to be pleasantly surprising. I gave them all my relevant points and facts, then let them handle the rest.

If you're banging your head against the wall trying to come up with the perfect bio, consider hiring a pro. They'll do it faster and let you get back to doing your other writerly things.

Recently, A.I. has come to the forefront of the publishing business, dividing authors into a few camps. One camp is all for the advancement of technology, embracing what A.I. can do to better our lives. The other camp is the polar opposite, viewing A.I. as a threat. Then, the last camp consists of people who are on the fence and don't really know much about it.

I encourage you to try generative A.I. in areas like drafting an author bio. You're ethically leveraging a tool to complete the sometimes-arduous task of describing yourself.

Google any number of text-generated A.I. services to see what's the best fit. At this time, you don't need to get a premium plan to craft a brief bio. Between ChatGPT and Dibbly Create, I have access to more than enough free-to-use generative A.I. to create a bio for myself anytime I want. I provide all the details to the A.I. and request an author bio with the specs I input. Then, hit enter. Within seconds, you should have a rough working bio. It might take a few tweaks or a couple of prompts to deliver a bio you can be proud of, but you can add your own touch without writing the bio from scratch.

YOUR AUTHOR BRAND IMAGE

Everyone judges a book by its cover; this is especially true with your author brand. You should present yourself, your work, and what you do in a cut and dry manner, right? Certainly, because you shouldn't be anything short of your authentic self.

However, you'll have to be self-aware and realize that most folks might not appreciate your authentic self. If you're the type who enjoys loafing around in your sweats and an unwashed T-shirt, then you probably shouldn't lead with that as your brand image.

Consider presenting yourself in your best casual attire, or if you want to project a professional image, opt for your Sunday best. In 2017, I stopped wearing business attire, such as pressed slacks, a long-sleeve shirt, tie with tie pin, and often a vest. I dressed that way for my career as an activities director. And, for a year after I left my job, I continued to use that as my look, even though I didn't really like it.

Instead of bothering myself with constantly wearing clothes that made me uncomfortable, I finally retired them to the back of my closet for good. I consciously chose an image that's casual yet put together. My normal everyday wear includes a T-shirt, jeans, and a pair of athletic shoes.

Every video I produce, every interview I conduct, and any appearance I make presents who I am in everyday life. Is this something you should do? That's entirely up to you. How you present yourself can limit your opportunities, so be mindful. Many conference promoters probably would pass on hiring me because I don't fit the more business-oriented look.

Am I worried about losing those opportunities? No. I'm sure I could make lucrative money if I chose that path, but at what expense? I'd be highly uncomfortable and would feel like I sacrificed who I am and what I'm all about.

DEVELOPING A PROFESSIONAL ONLINE PRESENCE

Over four years ago, my former video producer, Dan Norton, suggested a great idea. We found that every time I produced a video thumbnail—the graphic you see for a video on YouTube—with my orange T-shirt, we got better views and watch time. That night, I ordered five new orange T-shirts and have since ordered more.

Let's not just stop at how you look as an author. Let's focus on your actual body of work, from your books to your website to your social media presence.

Be consistent. First, you'll want to stick to one photo or professional headshot of you. Make sure people can clearly see your face. Also, it's a good idea to smile. It can be as subtle as you like. The exception to that rule would be horror authors or when smiling might seem contradictory to your niche.

A professional headshot by a seasoned photographer is always ideal if you can afford it. Should you not have the budget to hire a pro, then make do with what you have. The latest phones and tech can do the job.

Take a picture with you as the center of attention. Avoid having anything busy in your background. The latest iPhones have a neat feature called "cinematic" which lightly blurs the background. If you use that, make sure the effects are not junking up your image.

The key to a good headshot is you. Don't be modest about taking center stage. This is the image many people will come to know you by, so make it your best.

For a few bucks more, you can also take your DIY shot to a freelancer on Fiverr. They have some killer graphic design artists who can clean up your image and make it look really pro—all for about five bucks.

Once you have your best headshot, propagate it across every imaginable avenue you use. Your website, social media profile pics, author bio page for Amazon, and Goodreads are just a few examples of where to display your face.

Keep it consistent.

This might seem counter-intuitive since you want everyone to see all sides of you. Stick to one photo and be done with it for a while. The real magic happens when someone picks you out at a local conference. If you stick to the same look, you are easier to recognize.

One time, I was at a video creator conference when I heard a voice call from across the room. She quickly approached me, dressed to the tens and bubbling with enthusiasm. Her name was Shannon, and I couldn't for the life of me guess who she was and how she knew me. Apparently, she recognized me from my YouTube videos, so that was an ego stroke. But something was nagging at me; I somehow knew this woman.

The next day, I saw her again, but this time she was wearing fancy Lululemon clothing, a headband, and was sporting pigtails. Bingo! Shannon Vlogs! We'd crossed paths many times in a shared community with other video creators. I had seen her profile picture but had never really delved into who she was or what she did. Nevertheless, her profile image made a lasting impression.

Shannon is among my many close friends today, and she continues to rock it out as a content creator. This lasting connection came through the power of recognition and consistent branding.

This goes to show how important it is to be consistent and also present online or in-person. The more visible you are, the more likely people are to remember you and further cement a connection.

Another major part of your image is your books. I shouldn't have to repeat the adage; you know readers are going to judge your book by its cover design. You absolutely need a professional cover design for all your books. I've preached this repeatedly on YouTube, so I'll summarize what you should already know.

Your cover design is the greatest barrier of entry to success. Yes, you could be a phenomenal writer drafting out-of-this-world prose. However, few readers will buy your book if it doesn't look appealing enough. The issue with doing your own book cover is if you don't have the background or experience with typography, image choice, trends, and overall layouts, your DIY cover design might miss the mark.

There are a few exceptions to this rule—indie authors who make incredible cover designs—like Derek Murphy, Mandi Lynn, and more. For the rest of us, we need to lean on professional cover design services, so we don't waste our first impression on a half-assed cover.

You don't have to spend a whole lot of money since a pro book cover design can run from as little as $5 to $1000. Pricier doesn't always equate to better. In those cases, you're possibly paying more for an experienced pro with deeper insights into the business.

Should you choose a higher priced design service, check their portfolio first and cross-check with other authors. It's never enough to assume someone is giving you an accurate portfolio. Some freelance platforms don't fully vet their freelancers, so a few bad apples slip in.

As with your professional headshot, be consistent with the image on your books and overall branding. Your covers should have a similar layout, text, and overall feel to them. I often liken it to the hard rock band AC/DC. Within two notes of their songs, I know exactly who is playing. Yes, they write a variety of songs with different tempos and themes. But anytime I hear them, I know them by their trademark sound.

You want to capture the essence of your covers, then fill out the rest of your online presence with it. Get your website to match so when people land on your page, they know they're in the right place. Use images or graphics that support your cover design imagery through social media with banners or pinned posts. The sky is the limit, but just remember to keep it branded so you stay consistent.

You'll find a list of my preferred resources in the back of the book.

BUILDING A PRESS KIT

A press kit is a promotional tool that'll deliver massive value to your author brand. Whenever you get a booking, meet a new professional, or need to brag about who you are and what you do, the press kit is your answer.

In days past, people would build physical press kits that would include their headshot, short bio, and potentially a book or two. Today, you don't need to have a physical press kit, but you need a digital version.

Create a folder on your computer. Insert a copy of one or two of your best headshots, a few book covers, a sample of your content, and a bio sheet with all relevant links. Zip the folder and upload it to a cloud drive.

Then, create a direct download link. I recommend buying a domain name or using a redirect to send people to. Direct download links are often hard to remember and, without some brand recognition, hard to trust. I like the free WordPress service Pretty Links that uses my domain name plus a subdirectory to redirect traffic to my press kit.

For instance, I could host my press kit on my Google Drive, get the link, then have Pretty Links redirect with DaleLRoberts.com/PressKit. Any time someone visits that link, they get access to my press kit. Whenever I need to update my press kit with new headshots, images, or info, I start the process over again but replace the redirect link with the new one.

You get double points if you create a scannable QR Code that sends people to your press kit. Put it on your business card, in your books, and on your website. Of course, you don't need to make your press kit available to the public, it can be strictly for business professionals. Approach it as you see fit.

When meeting a person for the first time, instead of cramming a business card into their hands, chat them up and wait for the opportunity to mention your press kit if it makes sense. I typically reserve my press kit for potential interviews, speaking engagements, and appearances. Beyond that, it doesn't really apply anywhere else.

Set a reminder in your calendar every year to audit your press kit. No author stays the same for years at a time. You're going to publish more books, get more accolades, and grow as an author. Keep your press kit up to date.

For my bio, I use a free template through Canva. Anytime I need to update my bio, I log into Canva, make all the corrections, then update my press kit with the new bio sheet. Make your downloadable assets eye-catching and worth reading and looking at. That's why I use Canva to dress my bio sheet up to be more than just a Word document.

LEVERAGING SOCIAL MEDIA PLATFORMS FOR NETWORKING

Most of the information I've given so far implies in-person connections, but that's not mandatory. In fact, some of my best networking has come through social media. While we're talking about consistent author branding, we need to address the most massive opportunity in reach and brand growth.

Around 2018, I was kicking around on X (formerly known as Twitter), never truly taking it seriously. The site was merely my link dumping ground. X was a place for me to promote my videos and books; that was it. Little did I know I'd accumulate a small yet active following.

In my many interactions on the platform, I ran into another author, Kevin Tumlinson. We direct messaged each other a few times, and I discovered he was the Director of Marketing at the self-publishing service Draft2Digital. By being present and active on X, he and I fast became friends. This connection gave me insights and intel with the folks at Draft2Digital as they had new product rollouts and feature updates.

They've since been huge supporters and had me on their YouTube channel a couple of times to chat about self-publishing. The best part about that connection is it didn't cost me a dime, only time and one connection.

Never, ever take social media for granted. For whatever reason, I took X a bit more seriously after that interaction with Kevin. Our connection led to meeting even more fantastic business professionals who have changed my life in a big way.

Through Kevin Tumlinson, I met veteran internet marketer and business strategist, Jonny Andrews. Also, Kevin introduced me to the prolific author and my marketing copy go-to expert, Brian Meeks. Heck, I'm certain just knowing Kevin has been enough for folks to lay immediate trust in me. That's how respected he is.

Don't be mistaken. I'm not encouraging you to cover every imaginable social media platform. That's not a good use of your time. I've been down that dusty road before, and it's filled with nothing but heartaches and horse manure.

Pick one social media platform you enjoy or currently use. Some sites cater to specific tastes and interests, so be selective about where you go. As long as your ideal audience and peers reside there, it's probably a good place.

Don't let any online guru tell you one platform is better than the other. What makes the difference is where you can show up consistently and be present within your online community. Good marketing is all about visibility and that certainly applies to networking, too.

As you grow your business network, you're going to discover it's tough keeping up with everyone. One of the most efficient and easiest ways to keep up to date with your network is social media. You don't always have to send a DM, text, or email to be front of mind with your peers. Updating everyone on social media will go a long way.

In the early 2000s, I was a professional wrestler and made many lifelong friends and connections in that industry. Around 2011, I left the wrestling business because of my health, but I kept in touch with my connections online. One of my good friends is a world-traveled pro wrestler named Jake Crist. He and I always keep tabs on each other, so he knew a bit about what I'd been up to.

More recently, he went through an incredible transformation when he kicked a drinking habit and got himself into phenomenal shape. He found inspiration in his success and wanted to share his positive message throughout the world. So naturally, who did he contact? Me.

He'd followed me quite a bit on Instagram, noticing that I'm the guy who teaches people how to write and publish books. Even though it had been years since we last spoke, once he contacted me, we picked up right where we left off.

Never take the work you do on social media for granted. It can go a long way if you're truly invested and care about what you're doing and the people you connect with. You don't have to be perfect, but always calculate every action, engagement, or post. What you do reflects on your author brand. Do so with purpose and precision. What you post online can live for an eternity, so you must be careful about how you present yourself—at your best *and* worst.

We'll dive a little deeper into more practical steps for online networking strategies—what works and what has disastrous consequences.

CHAPTER 3
OFFLINE NETWORKING STRATEGIES

I have a surprising fact few people know about me, although I've mentioned it here—I'm an introvert. If left to my own devices, I'd much rather stay in the comfort of my home, entertaining myself with no outside interference. Is that healthy? Possibly not, especially if I want to pay those pesky things that come in the mail called bills.

Knowing my natural instincts limit my opportunities, I force myself to get out and meet new people. It sometimes comes with overwhelming anxiety and negative inner dialogue. Despite that hang-up, I push through because again, to build a ubiquitous author brand, I want to be visible.

Around 2019, my wife and I went to a book conference in Dayton where they hosted many free author panels and speakers. This event was the perfect space to learn about my industry from seasoned pros and, hopefully, to connect with a few.

One panel covered the importance of a professional cover design that included a few indie authors and the regional manager for a library chain. I found the talk enlightening and fun. Despite my inclination to be a wallflower, I asked questions and engaged in meaningful ways.

Detroit-based romance author Sylvia Hubbard was among the panel guests, and she made quite an impression with her keen insights and positive outlook. Little did I know she'd become one of my biggest supporters and collaborators on YouTube. Here's the funny part: we never directly exchanged phone numbers or details. I simply subscribed to her YouTube channel and followed her author profile on Amazon to get updates about her. We never even shook hands at the event, much less greeted each other.

When she commented on a video and reached out to me by email, I was shocked because here was this seasoned pro coming to ask me questions. We both had a good laugh when I'd shared how I'd seen her speak at the Dayton writer's conference. She vaguely remembered my face in the audience, but I definitely remembered her. We've since collaborated on a few videos, interviews, and online community events. I consider Sylvia one of my most trusted go-to authorities in the world of indie publishing and writing.

ATTENDING WRITING CONFERENCES AND LITERARY EVENTS

For anyone new to the writing and self-publishing business, going to in-person conferences and events can play a huge part in your continuing education. Counting on independent learning alone without a clear strategy might cause avoidable missteps when developing your author brand.

Around 2017, I started attending video creator conferences, hoping to level up my understanding of video production and YouTube. I had to go to every presentation. The ones I missed, I ear-marked to watch on the digital replay when I got home. I drove myself crazy running from one session to the next. After a half dozen conferences and running myself absolutely ragged, I gave myself permission to slow down, pick the most interesting presentations, then leave some wiggle room to meet new people or catch up with old friends.

While in-person conferences bring in big name experts and influencers who share their best strategies for business, countless more brilliant minds have their notepads ready to jot down ideas and concepts. Just because they're learning too doesn't mean they have nothing to offer.

The first year I went to VidSummit, a video creator conference based in Los Angeles, I met an online acquaintance, Dan Currier. He hosted a YouTube channel dedicated to sharing insights and strategies for YouTube. Though we knew of each other through a shared Facebook Group, we chatted like we'd known each other for years. Dan had about 500 subscribers, but he had the passion to really give this whole YouTuber thing the ol' college try.

Less than half a year later, his YouTube channel exploded because of one video he shot in his car. After that, he seemed to have the Midas touch, shooting videos that were pure gold for his audience. Naturally, we chatted occasionally, discussing his strategies, theories, and insights. A few years later, he launched a video creator conference out of Albany, New York, called People of Video.

While Dan was organizing the event, he'd briefly mentioned needing an emcee, so I jokingly offered my name. To my surprise, he didn't even hesitate and responded with a solid "yes." In the three years he ran People of Video, I was fortunate to take part in the show as an emcee and met some incredibly talented and well-versed folks in the video creator community.

None of this would've happened had I not slowed down at a conference and connected with someone. The biggest opportunity wasted at conferences is in not connecting with other attendees, as well as the presenters and speakers. Yeah, it feels pretty cool to have the attention of someone you admire, but it's even better when you realize they put their pants on one leg at a time like the rest of us.

If you're contemplating an in-person conference, factor in the expenses, but don't base your decision solely on the value of the speakers or presentations. Focus on the people attending the event, because these are people who have the same passion and drive as you. Surrounding yourself with great people raises you up to another level so that you grow with them.

Yes, in-person conferences can cost anywhere from free up to $1000 or more. Then, add the travel, hotel, food, and other accommodations and it can become pretty pricey. When looking at the value of an in-person event, you absolutely must factor in networking. For the past couple of years, when I've gone to in-person conferences, I've spent most of my time outside of the event—in the halls, at local restaurants, on walks, you name it.

I choose to make the most of my time by finding someone to talk to rather than being cooped up in a stuffy conference room or freezing in a massive ballroom. The challenge will come in stepping out beyond the people I know. If you're a wallflower like me, you'll probably avoid it at all costs. I encourage you to get a little uncomfortable and strike up a conversation with someone, anyone.

Two of the best opportunities exist when you're waiting for a speaker to begin or right after a talk. Look to either side of you and just choose someone to talk to. It's going to take one brave moment, but once you execute a simple question, the rest comes easy.

If you're nervous, it's totally fine. Start the conversation with that as a talking point; mention your excitement about being at the event. How you break the ice doesn't matter, as long as you start with a simple question and a brief introduction.

The conversation could go something like this:

Dale: Have you ever seen this speaker before?
Other person: [Insert answer]

Listen to the person and don't worry about a follow-up statement or force a handshake. I usually ask a few more questions to get to know the person a bit more. Once we've had a couple of exchanges, I might then ask their name and what they do. Being outside of a presentation serves you best in this situation because it allows you to have an uninterrupted talk with a newfound friend.

Should you not finish up the conversation as the presenter starts, ask to follow up with the person later in the hall or out for a coffee. People will rarely object to a low-stakes invitation like that; but if they bail without following up, it's no big deal because there are a ton of other attendees who'll chat you up.

When you meet someone, track their name, what they do, and how you can contact them. Do not rely on your memory, because after a three- to five-day conference, you'll probably be on information overload and will be less able to retain all the finer details. I always have my Notes app open on my iPhone so I jot down info easily, including what a person looks like, so it makes for quick and easy recall.

It's not enough for you to leave the conference and never talk to your connections again. For every ten people I connect with at a conference, only a few contacts stay in touch. It doesn't reflect poorly on those business professionals. For whatever reason, they have the discretionary time to chat with their peers at a conference, but once you introduce them back into their normal routine, it's easy to lose track of those new connections.

This shouldn't be the case for you. Take the initiative in maintaining communications after the conference, whether through a friendly follow-up email or an invitation to video chat. A little goes a long way, so don't feel obligated to spend countless hours chatting or drafting the perfect email.

For example:

Hey, Dan,

It was super cool getting connected at VidSummit. I'd love to stay in touch and learn a little more about what you've got going on. Do you have any availability next week to chat over a virtual cup of coffee?

If there are relevant details you got about them in a conversation, mention it. People like to know you're listening and care about them. Should the other person ghost you, don't take it personally. Move on. You might cross paths again later. I'm not a fan of hounding someone like they owe me money. The choice is simple: either they want to connect or they do not.

With the number of people in and around this business, you have an endless supply of potential peers for your network. It's *not* the end of the world if one person wants to connect with you more than someone else. Think less of it like dating and more like an open conversation with the world.

Managing your contacts is going to require a lot of diligence. I use the Contacts feature in Gmail to track all the folks I meet. That's why I lean on email for communicating with other business professionals. It also helps me track conversations and threads so I don't forget what we talked about last. How you store this is completely up to you, as long as you do it.

Worst-case scenario: You attend an in-person event and leave with no contacts—don't sweat it. You'll get another chance to connect with other people now that you have previous conference experience to share.

Let's assume you have little money to attend these premium events. What are the other options?

LOCAL WRITING GROUPS AND WORKSHOPS

My wife, Kelli, is always on the lookout for free community events and volunteer opportunities. She's attended and even worked at local races, taco fests, and even some book clubs. Kelli loves the challenge of finding free events that deliver on a premium level. Should the event be a bust, she always chalks it up to experience and getting to meet new people.

Recently she found our favorite local restaurant and bookstore was hosting a new monthly event called *Shut Up and Write*. Because she's subscribed to a website called Meetup.com, she gets alerts about interesting local events. We were even more interested because *Shut Up and Write* was completely free.

The premise for this meetup was to dedicate an hour to writing. The time before and after the event was open for chatting with other authors. We attended the event a few times and were quite productive while getting to meet other online entrepreneurs.

Finding free events is really quite easy—Google. When I'm looking for a new event or meetup, I look up free events in the Columbus area. Or I monitor my local libraries or coffee shops. Some event hosts want to draw in more traffic, so the easiest way to do that is hosting a free event.

Kelli and I with our friend Helen Kinson had arranged a few local meetups for online entrepreneurs. We had three separate meetups at a couple of different local restaurants. I've spent thousands on conferences and had a blast of a time, but none of those compare to small get-togethers, especially when they are free.

Sure, you could make the argument that you still have to buy food when you host in-person events. If you want to offer a completely free event, look into local libraries and coffee shops. A few places don't require you to spend money, as long as you are polite and encourage your attendees to support the host location however they can. For some meetings we hosted, a few attendees didn't buy a thing, yet the hosts weren't at all upset. Again, some traffic for them is better than no traffic at all.

Libraries are probably the best resources for local workshops and free conferences. To foster community involvement, libraries often have to host a rotating schedule of events and activities while operating on a limited budget. It's the library's mission to enrich the surrounding community. The first best thing for you to do is sign up for an email list for your local library or pop in to get a monthly events calendar to see what's coming that may be of interest. And, since you're an author, it's probably a good idea to be visible at your local library, because that could pay off in a big way.

As for free events beyond libraries, the Dayton book conference where I first saw Sylvia Hubbard was free. The event organizers likely covered the costs through vendor fees and sponsorship revenue, allowing me to have fun without the worry of paying a premium for admission. My wife and I had a blast, got to see some great booths, and enjoyed a few excellent talks about the world of writing and publishing.

JOINING AUTHOR ASSOCIATIONS AND ORGANIZATIONS

When in doubt about where to go and when, consider author associations and organizations. They're great conduits for networking. Some will host events and conferences, while others will recommend events for authors.

Be aware that most author organizations charge membership fees, usually through annual dues. Though I have recommendations in the resources section, I'll still discuss a few of the best organizations here.

When searching for an author association, focus on your niche. For instance, if you're a horror writer, consider the Horror Writers Association. Or, if you're a sci-fi fantasy author, consider the Science Fiction & Fantasy Writers Association. You will still find value in larger, more general conferences like Author Nation or the Self-Publishing Show Live. The more general conferences will often have panels or presentations about craft, but that isn't what the whole conference is about.

Think about what makes the most sense from a business perspective when selecting events to attend. Should you go to a massive live event that broadly covers author-related topics, it's not a bad thing. You just might find more value in a niche event since you'll meet folks walking the same path as you. When you match yourself up with authors writing in your genre, you might find doors open that lead to more collaborative opportunities.

While the large events have an enormous pool of attendees to network, not all of them will be a good fit. Whereas smaller events, specifically meant for a niche, provide a deeper pool of relevant attendees who might be perfect to add to your business network.

As long as you're trying to get out from behind your desk and into the real world to make truly lasting connections, it's a win. You don't have to go to every conference and event out there. Be selective with your time because the more you spend at a conference, the less you spend on your author business. My limit is four premium conferences per year. Free events are okay, as long as travel expenses are within my budget.

Don't forget to track all expenses related to attending these events, including tickets, food, hotel, mileage, and any other travel-related items. Report these items in your annual tax filing. I provide my certified public accountant (CPA) with all that information, and it goes a long way in reducing the amount I owe in taxes every year. Speak to your local CPA about how this benefits your business.

When in-person conferences bring out a crippling amount of agoraphobia, what should you do? Just suck it up and hope you don't get a panic attack? Well, no!

Thankfully, we're in a digital age where you can get all you need from the comforts of your home. That's why online networking is possibly the easiest way to build your network and possibly the most effective way I've grown my network of business professionals.

CHAPTER 4
ONLINE NETWORKING STRATEGIES

Every author, regardless of their experience or success, benefits from leveraging online networking opportunities. Unlike in-person networking events, you don't have to pay for travel expenses and, sometimes, you won't even have to pay for admission. You don't even have to leave your home.

From the standpoint of saving time and money while reaping nearly the same rewards as in-person networking, online networking is the best option. The only real problem is deciding where to go, what you should do, and how you can best leverage online networking to grow your author brand.

In-person connections have a distinct feeling about them, an almost unseen synergistic energy exchange by being in contact with another human. I leave that up to the scientists to prove or disprove. For me, it's always more fun and exhilarating when I'm at an in-person event.

That's not to take anything away from online networking. There's still a bit of an energy exchange, but it's not as visceral as what you get in person. Don't stress over that detail because you can maximize this avenue even if you never take part in another face-to-face event.

CHAPTER 4: ONLINE NETWORKING STRATEGIES

VIRTUAL CONFERENCES, LIVE STREAMS, AND SOCIAL MEDIA

Oh. My. Lord. Just how many virtual conferences have sprung up over the past five years? There was a veritable tsunami of virtual events once the pandemic hit in early 2020. The popularity continued to grow and so did the pockets of event hosts. Certain conferences were premium, while others followed a freemium model—offering free access with the option to upgrade for exclusive perks.

I truly believe these online events can be incredible. I've attended so many of these that I could write an entire book about it—please, don't tempt me. I've experienced the good, the bad, and the ugly as a featured guest.

Keep an eye out for online events that connect attendees through a shared community—be it a forum, group page, or live video chat. These are the ones worth exploring because they offer the opportunity to connect with like-minded business professionals. Often, the only way to know if an event has that option is if you ask.

Remember my old friend Dan Currier? The first year of his conference, People of Video, things didn't go as planned. In late March 2020, most of the U.S. went into lockdown, forcing Dan to find an alternative for his in-person event.

He had no choice but to either refund all his attendees' fees or offer a virtual conference as a suitable replacement. Thankfully, People of Video's virtual event was a smashing success with dozens of amazing experts contributing incredible presentations.

As part of the event, attendees got early access to the event through a kick-off party hosted through a Zoom video chat. A few dozen bright-eyed and bushy-tailed people showed up. Everyone seemed super happy to be there, and what happened next forever changed my mind about how impactful virtual events can be.

Dan planned at least two hours for a networking mixer. He divided the attendees into separate rooms. Each person would introduce themselves and then select the next person to speak. Once we got our introductions in, we'd talk shop about video creation strategies, branding, and other best practices. As soon as our time was up, Dan mixed up the order and threw everyone into different virtual rooms again, starting the cycle over.

Though not everyone met everybody, that mixer fostered enough connections to last everyone for years to come.

Until that day, I didn't know Zoom had the option to separate guests into individual virtual rooms. In fact, I later did the same thing when I gathered some of my closest friends and peers who are in the video content space for writing and self-publishing.

What made the experience so game-changing was not just having the opportunity to chat with other folks but being forced to interact with others. I never regretted it because I walked away with new contacts and a fun story to share.

The one luxury I have in going to in-person events is that I never really have to talk to anyone. I can hang back, scope things out, and bolt if I'm not feeling it.

In a virtual networking mixer? No chance! Once I'm committed to a virtual mixer, I don't feel right about just bailing, so I'll stick around for the entire meeting.

All you have to do is show up. Make sure your webcam is clean, your mic picks up your voice, and be considerate of everyone else's time.

Whenever I feel like I'm talking too much, I involve someone else with a question. Asking a simple question can easily get a conversation going, fostering a more inclusive environment for everyone.

Be selective with what you ask, so avoid hot-button issues or incendiary topics. Otherwise, you should be good, as long as you're keeping the conversation going or contributing in some small way.

If you're comfortable being on camera, then look into live streaming and video content creation. I only started interviewing guests on my channel because I wanted to learn from them. Rather than be selfish and keep those lessons to myself, I shared them with the world.

Little did I know that some of my greatest accomplishments and connections would come by simply asking for an interview. To date, I've interviewed over 125 guests in the writing and self-publishing space. Staggering, to be honest. You don't have to follow in my footsteps; I'm merely illustrating one path to consider.

My buddy and fellow YouTuber, Shanon "S.D." Huston is a great example of someone blazing her own trail. She's hosted two virtual conferences and dozens of collaborative live streams with other authors. You don't have to know who is on the stream, because it comes off as a relaxed conversation among friends. They're networking in front of a live audience around the world.

They could offer that same video meetup as a private gathering. Instead, they bring other viewers from various channels, creating an even deeper sense of community. You don't have to be on the live video to enjoy the experience thoroughly, with viewers having the ability to contribute through live chats, polls, or even through direct interaction with the stars.

While commenting may not seem like much to a viewer, it truly means the world to video creators. I've made a few digital acquaintances through live streaming videos. I recognize their names and their profile pictures and that creates a connection.

If you are a video content creator, it'll be up to you to take that first step and reach out. Scout other channels like yours on YouTube, Twitch, TikTok, Instagram, or Facebook. Support the creators you enjoy the most and contribute however you can. When the time is right, ask them if they'd be interested in co-hosting a live stream or collaborating on a video.

You can contact a video creator two ways—through the comments section or searching for their email address. I prefer to approach other creators about business through an email. Posting a request in the comments of a video may come across as needy to others. I usually comment when I really enjoy a video and never try to take the spotlight away from the creator.

Once you get the opportunity, show up with your A-game and have fun! Viewers who see you having fun will most likely enjoy themselves too. Don't be afraid to cut up, but keep it dialed in enough that you maintain your professionalism.

ENGAGING WITH WRITING COMMUNITIES AND FORUMS

Between Facebook Groups, Discord Communities, and online forums, authors have an endless sea of options to choose from. I recommend being part of at least one online community, especially one focused on your niche.

Facebook alone has thousands of groups for authors that cover any niche or need out there. Consider book clubs, writing masterminds, and all things related to becoming a better indie author. Search on Facebook, filter the options to the groups, and take your pick.

A huge reason I pivoted to Discord was its lack of preferential algorithmic treatment. You don't need to get a bunch of engagement for people to notice your comments or posts. I wanted to make a safe space where authors could connect with other authors. Discord is a free-to-use site where you can grow a community and connect with your audience. When members visit the community, they're not subject to the whims of an algorithm. Instead, they get equal access to public threads and get to choose what they want to read or chat about.

Think of Discord like an all-you-can-eat buffet—you'll get many options in a single community, but you don't need to try them all. You get to dictate what you see and when you see it.

You'll find plenty of options, but you never have to settle for just one. It's a good idea to be active in at least one, so you have your pulse on the scene and remain visible in the community. Eventually, you will need to contribute, so approach it like a casual, yet professional, conversation.

If you check in at least once a day and contribute in some meaningful way, more folks are apt to connect with you.

Once you've had quite a few interactions with other community members, see if anyone would like to meet for a virtual meetup. You can chat about business or many topics relevant to the community. Be specific about when and where the meetup will happen. Zoom, Google Meet, and Discord offer a space for group video chats for free.

Should you not want to organize a virtual meetup, ask if anyone knows of one you could join. No one can fault you for asking, so try that if you don't want to be the organizer.

COLLABORATING WITH OTHER AUTHORS ON PROJECTS

The greatest untapped resource in all of self-publishing is author collaborations. Hundreds of thousands of authors currently work together through co-authoring books, newsletter swaps, and group promos. Yet that's nothing compared to the number of authors in self-imposed seclusion.

You can be successful on your own, yet you increase the likelihood and shorten your timeline when working with other authors. While the rising tide raises all boats, your boat has to be in the same harbor as the others.

Though I've studied co-authoring books in great detail, I'm far from being the go-to authority in this area. From what I've learned, all authors should proceed in co-authoring books with caution. Once you create a money-generating asset with another business professional, you're stuck with them indefinitely (or for an agreed-upon timeframe). Not to mention that writing styles can clash or the project might not come out as brilliantly as expected.

Save co-authoring for authors you truly know and trust. I'm fortunate the founder of Book Launchers, Julie Broad, wrote the foreword for my nine-time award-winning book, *The Amazon Self Publisher*. I'd known her for a few years, so I was fairly comfortable asking after quite a few video collaborations and virtual meetups. I wouldn't have asked her if I believed she'd do a terrible job or make the writing process difficult.

For my book *Self-Publishing for New Authors*, I leaned on my buddy and YouTube content creator, Keith Wheeler. He was one of my first coaching students, so I've watched him grow an incredible brand, assisting authors while publishing a variety of children's books and nonfiction books. After getting to know Keith through coaching, I knew he was the best person for the job and would be an asset to my next publication. He gladly obliged and I'm sure that has a lot to do with staying connected, being of service to him, and asking for a favor when the time was right.

Premium book marketing services like StoryOrigin and BookFunnel act as an author marketplace where collaborations happen through newsletter swaps and group promos. These service providers give authors a space to meet with other authors without the awkwardness of person-to-person contact.

For newsletter swaps, two authors agree to share each other's book in their respective email newsletters. It's an ethical quid pro quo system as long as you're collaborating with authors that produce the same type of content you do. A bad newsletter swap would be if a romance author collaborates with a self-help author. Both audiences would be confused, and the authors could lose a few email subscribers.

Group promos are like a newsletter swap on steroids. A collection of authors promotes all their books through a special discount or niche-specific showcase. Each author drives traffic to the deal, thus pooling their resources to get better results.

Before you agree to any collaborations, make sure you fully vet who you work with. First, read their content so you can confidently stand behind their books. Next, check out how they handle themselves online and in public. Social media is revealing in that way, so you'll know if someone is a good fit or not. Last, only collaborate with an author if it makes sense to you.

It's okay to feel a little weird if you're new to author collaborations, especially if you've never met the author. Newsletter swaps and group promos are an entry point to potentially more networking opportunities like video interviews or co-authoring.

If you organized one newsletter swap per week for a year, that'd give you fifty-two different authors who have advocated for you. That goodwill goes a long way should you ever want to level up your networking game. Now, imagine having a book launch and all fifty-two authors promoted it.

That's just a rough example of what is possible through author collaborations. You're only limited by your imagination and your willingness to work with others. If that's a tall ask, then start with one and work your way up to more.

USING ONLINE PLATFORMS FOR BOOK PROMOTION AND NETWORKING

Networking with no motive is totally fine, but let's be honest, no one wants to just make friends and *possibly* sell books. When you're connecting with other authors or online entrepreneurs, you want it to be a meaningful relationship that's mutually beneficial. You don't have to feel manipulative for wanting something out of a relationship, especially if you're willing to give more than you get.

Reciprocity is not mandatory, but you'll know the folks who are grateful for your help in a time of need and those who expect you to give help. You'll never know until you try, but one of the best ways to tell if someone is reliable is through a referral or introduction.

Timing is everything when asking for a favor or requesting help from a network peer. Asking too many times in too close a period could be a major turnoff, costing you any real leverage for future help.

Once you've established a presence through online communities and been of assistance to your network, lean on them for outside help when you need it most. Whether you're launching a book or running a price promotion for your backlog, tapping into your network for help is a small ask.

Just be prepared to return the favor at a future date so you become a reliable peer in your business network. With all the opportunities you have through the various avenues previously mentioned, you'll have more than enough chance to promote your book to the moon and back.

CHAPTER 5
EFFECTIVE COMMUNICATION AND RELATIONSHIP BUILDING

I felt horrified, embarrassed, and rather clumsy after making one big mistake networking. Introducing two authors from within my network seemed like a win for everyone. Two of my author friends, Joe and Raul, were a couple of my absolute favorite people. On paper, the two seemed to be a great match. They were both full-time authors, had established brands, and, to me, they had similar outlooks on the writing and publishing business.

Joe was a video content creator who'd interviewed several brilliant authors and experts. Raul was always looking for interview opportunities so he could get his name out more and meet new people. Instantly, my gut told me it was a lock. Joe and Raul could be the best of friends, so why not make an introduction? Joe could use a guest for his video interviews, and Raul would have additional exposure through an interview. Not to mention the lifelong camaraderie we'd all have where we'd laugh at inside jokes, grow our businesses together, and continue to meet and share new people.

Yeah, that didn't happen at all. In fact, what really happened took the wind out of me and left me in a state of utter shock. All I did was introduce the two authors through email. I sang their praises, explained the opportunity I saw, and let them take it from there. Only a couple of weeks later, I received a scathing message from Raul.

"Hey, Dale, I appreciate the referral to Joe, but please, in the future, could you clear it with me beforehand as opposed to a blind introduction?"

Oh, there was more, because Raul had me dead to rights. Think about it from his perspective. Imagine you're minding your own business, then someone randomly introduces you to some stranger, then splits. How would you feel about it? Unintentionally, I had indirectly communicated that Raul's time was mine to use as I saw fit. He had no say in the matter.

I essentially said, "Here you go, Raul! I know you're not busy and even if you are, it's not as important as talking to this guy I've never told you about."

As it turned out, Joe had confirmed the scheduled interview time earlier in the day but had to cancel because of a personal emergency a half hour before the meeting. When Raul found out what the pressing issue was, he became furious because he didn't think it was a justifiable reason to call off at the last minute.

Unbeknownst to me, Raul had already heard some bad things about Joe being flaky and sketchy. To be clear, I never knew Joe had any issues, so what Raul shared with me was hearsay. Yet I couldn't invalidate the way he felt about Joe. That ship had already sailed well before this introduction.

Joe was apologetic with me, explaining that his family dog had become violently ill, so he'd had to rush to the vet. It was an unfortunate situation made worse by my good intentions.

Indeed, the road to hell is paved with good intentions. My blunder affected three authors negatively—Joe, Raul, and me.

I love making introductions to people within my network of business professionals. When I introduce one professional to another, their collective pool of resources shoots up. By making these introductions, each professional can refer cross-traffic, exponentially increasing their respective reach.

Had I laid the groundwork with both authors, the execution would have been fine, and we could have completely avoided the entire ordeal. If I had laid the groundwork with both authors before ever making an introduction, I could have averted the crisis. Rather than impulsively introducing two network professionals, I should've started with getting permission, confirming it with both parties, then making the introduction.

Not everyone has the time or mental bandwidth to meet and interact with new people, regardless of how excited I am to introduce them. By blindly setting up an introduction, I forcibly took time from both parties without their consent. It wasn't just my email introduction alone, but I hadn't considered both men needing time to connect and get to know each other.

Any sense of reservation or apprehension is completely valid when you think about the ugly situation I just shared. The sad part is the incident could've been a lot worse. With time and practice, you too can introduce peers within your network, but you will need the best practices and the unspoken etiquette of networking.

CHAPTER 5: EFFECTIVE COMMUNICATION AND RELATIONSHIP BUILDING

NETWORKING ETIQUETTE & BEST PRACTICES

Should you really be reading how to conduct yourself as a professional who's looking to grow a business and build an author brand? No, but the old phrase holds true:

Common sense isn't always common practice.

As much as I don't like this rather abrasive quote, it applies in so many walks of business and in life. Common sense would've dictated that I got permission from Joe and Raul to make the introduction. I could've avoided the whole calamity. Yet I allowed my impulse to get the best of me and threw common sense out the window.

The next thing is to never get too comfortable.

I spoke at a conference once where they had an open bar for VIP attendees and speakers. The event organizer brought us all into a crammed room where we all gobbled down tasty hors d'oeuvres and shared in fun conversation. An open bar indicates you can drink all you want, but should you? One speaker drank a few too many. Within one hour, he was loud, overbearing, and downright uncomfortable to be around.

I saw my way out of the event, ready to get away from the drunken fool who didn't have enough sense to limit his alcohol intake. A few other attendees reflected later on how obnoxious the man got and the amount he drank.

I'm sure he meant well, or he might even have an alcohol dependency. Regardless of why this happened, he got a little too comfortable. Getting inebriated at a business event is not an endearing trait, so he lost quite a few potential contacts and tons of respect for his blunder. There's no telling what opportunities he squandered by letting his inner fraternity bro out.

When you're meeting other business professionals, lead with your best self. Consider it a first date every time; dress to impress and lead with your best behavior. What you do and say can and will be used against you, so be professional at all times. I'm not implying that you cannot be your true and authentic self, but you darn sure better not be leading with some questionable behavior and polarizing language.

INTRODUCTIONS & ENGAGEMENT

When first meeting someone, get a read on what the situation calls for. You don't want to blast someone with your name right away with no real icebreaker dialogue that'd justify the introduction.

For in-person introductions, consider a simple handshake and request the other person's name and what they do. Sit back and just listen. Take any mental notes you can and allow the other person time to share about themselves. Usually, they'll follow up with questions about you, and thankfully, you already have your little elevator pitch ready to go.

Once you're done, follow up with another question whether it applies to you or applies to the other speaker. You get bonus points if you can combine the information about you and your peer to create a thought-provoking question that'll keep the conversation going. The key is to have back-and-forth exchanges.

You really have to stop and get to know the other person, even if you only have a few minutes. People love when you slow down and truly want to talk beyond surface level banter. Effective networking is essentially friendship building.

I don't expect you to go into every conversation with an overwhelming desire to get matching tattoos. At the very least, walk away from each interaction with the person's name and what they do. How they work within your network won't reveal itself until it's 100% necessary. That time might be right away or years later, you never can tell.

Follow up with anyone you connected with. That person might be interesting, charismatic, insightful, or whatever else tickles your fancy. I prefer emails, but you'll need to find out what they prefer when initially chatting.

"What's the best way to contact you? I might have something in the pipeline later on, so I want to make sure I get it to you STAT."

You're not asking someone on a date, so don't let fear get in the way of asking. In a lot of cases, if the other person doesn't want to be contacted, you'll sense it. Or, they'll just come right out and say it.

If you're at a local business meetup or mixer, chances are likely the other person is going to give their card. Take the card and store it away for safekeeping.

Before you lock that business card into a vault, store the contact info away in a digital folder. I use Gmail Contacts, again, for this task. Place additional notes on the contact that'll help with memory recall later.

For instance:

Bob Robbins was the guy in the neon pink business suit at the Chamber of Commerce meeting on September 9, 2023. We talked about his offset printing service based in Phoenix, Arizona.

Any time I get a business card I wanted, I'll follow-up with an email within the first day or so. Think of it like thanking someone for coming to your birthday party. Make it light, reinforce what you spoke about, and keep the conversation going.

Occasionally, I dip into my list of contacts and reach out to someone I haven't heard from in a while. It's always fun hearing what they've been up to since we last connected. It further merits a meetup, whether in-person or through video chat, even if for fifteen to thirty minutes. I always think about what I can do to be of service to somebody else.

It's not something I'd execute on first contact, more so after I've gotten to know and trust someone. On LinkedIn, I used to get a lot of direct messages of folks who'd skip right to the "I'd like to be of service to you." They'd come in hot with their first DM, introducing themselves, sharing how they loved my content, and then would jump right into service mode.

Why? I didn't even know them, so why were they trying to do things for me despite us never sharing a single word with each other? It comes off as weird and slightly manipulative from the perspective of a complete stranger. This rushed offer to help seems out of left field and appears suspicious. Don't offer help unless you have established a connection and built trust.

Trust doesn't come from cold prospecting clients in their DMs on social media. It comes from genuine interactions between real people.

Sadly, a lot of these best practices and etiquette come with time and practice. You're going to step on some toes at first and you'll know when you do. Just be self-aware enough to recognize your mistakes and do your best to avoid them in the future.

While I could give you a few more scenarios to be wary of, the real lesson reads like this:

> *Be excellent to each other.*
> *-Bill & Ted's Excellent Adventure*

You should know when you're being good because it'll come out in how you interact with business professionals. If your network is growing, chances are likely you're doing something right. Remember, slow growth is still growth just the same. If you find your network shrinking, re-evaluate how you're conducting yourself or the people you are engaging with.

You're going to have to kiss a few frogs before you find your one true prince, the same way you're going to meet some people that you won't want to associate with. You don't need to make it a big thing, simply cut ties and move on. Should that person try to eke their way back into your life, establish some boundaries and proceed with caution.

For instance, a podcast host invited me for an interview on her channel. The entire process leading up to the interview was aggravating because the interviewer and her assistant bombarded me with tons of demands and requests. When the day came, I had the worst experience. The host talked a lot, interrupted me when I was answering her questions, and even closed out her show asking me if I had questions for her.

What?! I thought. *You're not my guest; I'm your guest.*

To say the least, I was absolutely done working with this woman. Her assistant contacted me again, wanting to schedule another interview because the host enjoyed me so much. I'm sure she's a sweet woman with great intentions, but neither one of us benefit from this exchange anymore because:

1. I'd be less likely to cooperate in the interview.
2. She'd have a pretty tough time.

Despite her best efforts, no one wins there. Going into another unpleasant situation like that makes no sense.

I didn't have to confront the host or send a demeaning or demoralizing response to the assistant. I simply responded with appreciation for the second opportunity but politely declined. I further expressed my gratitude and wished her the best of luck.

That's it. I didn't burn any bridges and hurt no one's feelings.

Being your authentic self doesn't mean having to subject yourself to torture through less than desirable situations with people who don't align with you. You simply can't please everyone, so focus on the few you can, and build even deeper and more meaningful connections.

BUILDING GENUINE CONNECTIONS WITH INDUSTRY PROFESSIONALS

If I had to do it all over again, I would've been a lot more deliberate about introducing Joe and Raul. In my heart, I believe they would've gotten along just fine, but since Raul had already heard bad things about Joe, I faced an uphill battle.

The best step forward would've been to contact Joe first, asking him if he wanted any new guests. I'd wait for the all-clear before suggesting my buddy Raul. At that point, I could've shared Raul's books, his interviews, and his website. If I got the all-clear from Joe, then I'd go to Raul and do the same thing with him. I'd share Joe's videos, books, and website.

I feel fairly confident Raul would've been honest with me and told me any reservations he had about Joe by then. If that had been the case, I wouldn't have made the introduction. Had Raul given the green light for the introduction and then expressed his concerns about Joe, that would've been on Raul, not me. Despite how this turned out, I did not disown Joe and Raul. In fact, I've kept in touch with both authors since this happened.

The business professionals in your network will have to be civilized adults despite bad situations or confrontations. You're not there to choose sides or be their mediator. I promise you will run into issues with people you know not liking each other. Do your best to stay out of it and express your neutrality when parties want you to weigh in.

Though it rarely happens, it's still a possibility. This means you should spend the majority of your time connecting with more business professionals and readers. Notice I added your reading audience to the mix. No matter the number of readers following you, you have an additional connection to leverage for growing your author brand reach.

As authors, we're in a position to build advance reader copy (ARC) teams who'll read your book ahead of a release, then drop a review upon launch. We can also work with beta readers, your most dedicated and die-hard fans willing to give feedback on early versions of our manuscript, further helping with development so the manuscript is near perfect before copy editing.

Then, you've got the elite reader who's willing to join your digital street team, the folks responsible for marketing and promoting your book launches and backlog.

How crazy is that? To not consider your readership as part of your network would be foolish. They're probably going to be the best contacts in your network. Will you need the same approach with these reader groups as you will with traditional networking contacts? That's entirely up to you, but you could easily communicate with your ARC, beta reading, and street teams through any email marketing service like MailerLite, ConvertKit, MailChimp, and more.

Be prepared to volley emails from time to time with your readers. Replying to readers builds a deeper connection, and signals to your reader a willingness to listen and be heard. That fosters trust, an integral part of any relationship. Should you find reader emails are clouding up your day, consider a policy around how and when you'll respond while sharing your gratitude for them being a reader.

I have a one-email rule for readers that contact me. Many business professionals simply ignore emails they feel aren't worth their time, while others don't even care about their email inboxes. Not me. I like to keep a clear inbox while still maintaining a connection with my readers and peers. When I get a bit too busy, I simply give a response and follow it up with the next best step.

Feel free to join me in my community if you have any additional questions.

- *Discord - DaleLinks.com/Discord*

This mitigates any time loss from answering questions one-on-one that aren't in the confines of paid coaching. As you can

CHAPTER 5: EFFECTIVE COMMUNICATION AND RELATIONSHIP BUILDING

imagine, I get a ton of questions by email and DMs. Thanks for your understanding.

I gave them an answer and provided them with additional options that may help them resolve their issues. Is this a realistic approach for everyone? No, because your schedule, free time, and mental bandwidth differ completely from mine.

Whenever my schedule gets slammed, I have a less happy option for my readers.

Unfortunately, due to the large volume of emails and direct messages, I'm unable to respond to everyone. Sadly, I'm also not accepting new clients because of my heavier than normal workload.

Feel free to join me in my communities at…

The best part about each interaction is that I'm actually responding and providing an option. That is better than radio silence, or worse yet, a rude retort. Not everyone knows what your life is like beyond writing and publishing books. Every person draws a different version of you in their minds. That's not in your hands, so should someone be rude to you, block them and move on.

Another benefit of these types of responses is that I funnel each person into my communities on Facebook or on Discord. This means they'll land in a spot where other authors are happy to help because they've been in their shoes too. I treat people who email me with kindness, so they pay that kindness forward. While Facebook isn't the greatest for overall community engagement, it still functions fairly well in gathering like-minded people in one spot. On Discord, community members are overwhelmingly supportive and eager to answer questions or concerns.

Interacting with your readers and followers should work the same as it does for business professionals. Just remember to show tact, professionalism, and poise so you ensure that relationship stays around for the long run.

CHAPTER 6
LEVERAGING TECHNOLOGY FOR NETWORKING

Though we briefly touched on the use of technology for online networking, let's take a deeper look into a few ways you can better use modern tech to connect with your network—whether business professionals or your readers. After all, the old-fashioned methods of staying in contact are great, but if you plan to build a massive network to last for the long haul, tech is more efficient and practical.

While some recommendations seem obvious, a few authors choose to avoid them because of fear of extra work or a concern that learning technology will take them out of their normal author routines. I'm not trying to load your already full plate with a bunch of dead-end busywork. I'm aiming to make networking much easier so you have more time to write and promote your author brand.

USING EMAIL MARKETING TO CONNECT WITH YOUR NETWORK

Every author should have an email list since that's one of the greatest ways to retain your reading audience. Having an email list is akin to insurance because it protects you in the event of a wrongful account termination or deplatforming. Now, don't assume only incendiary and polarizing celebrities and public figures are targets for platform removal. Even some of the most honest authors have had the misfortune of losing access to their publishing or social media accounts.

Quite a few years ago, I knew of a highly successful indie publishing romance author who was pulling in six-figures per month in earnings. He was doing it all by simply publishing and enrolling his ebooks into Kindle Direct Publishing (KDP) and the KDP Select Program. Though he could've made a premium in print and audio book sales, he stuck to what was making him the most revenue—ebooks.

He was so singular in his focus that he never created a website, social media presence, or email list. This man was drawing thousands of new readers every month, so he assumed his ride would last forever. After all, nothing can go wrong if you're driving massive sales and revenue through Amazon, right?

Wrong!

In one fell swoop, KDP terminated his account for reasons he never understood. Because he only published ebooks, those all vanished overnight, leaving no trace of his work on Amazon. If he had print books, the product detail pages would have remained for third party sellers. And, had he published audiobooks, the KDP account termination would've never affected that platform.

All that aside, lacking print and audio versions of his books was the least of his worries. He lost his entire reading audience. Unless he scrambled to whip together a website at the last minute, there'd have been no way for his readers to find him, much less know he existed.

CHAPTER 6: LEVERAGING TECHNOLOGY FOR NETWORKING

Even a website whipped together hastily didn't mean that his readers could find a brand-new site that had zero search engine relevance.

He was at the top of the world; and if he'd only had an email list of his readers, he'd have lost so much less. I felt bad for him.

With email marketing services like MailerLite, ConvertKit, Mailchimp, and more, you have a variety of options, especially if you have no money to invest. Those three email marketing services provide free access up to a certain number of subscribers before charging. Though this chapter isn't going to dive deep into how to set up an account and manage it, I'll give you enough information to make you dangerous—in a good way.

To simplify building an email list, you'll want to:

1. Select your email marketing service.
2. Create a landing page for readers to opt into your email newsletter.
3. Share the link to the landing page everywhere—in your book, on social media, in your email signature, and so on.

While an email list might not be as practical for networking with business professionals, it can work if you're growing such a massive database of business professionals that it's becoming nearly impossible to communicate with everyone efficiently.

A few years ago, I took an inventory of how many friends and peers I knew in the YouTube space who were closely involved with writing and publishing. I've always enjoyed getting together with other people doing the same thing I am and brainstorming various strategies and theories to success. I had a list of over fifty video content creators sharing roughly the same niche.

The issue was emailing every one of them, especially if I wanted to meet up with this crew more than just once. Though it was a grind, I painstakingly contacted every one of them to present them with the idea of a monthly mastermind for video creators.

My hard work paid off because everyone got back to me in some capacity. Most of the folks shared how meeting up monthly would have a lot to do with timing. Organizing a monthly meetup at the right time for over fifty people is an impossible task. If I had even a quarter of them attend, it would have been a success.

The one thing I recommended to them in my first communication was to join an email newsletter since I was organizing such a massive group and could update everyone on the best times and video chat links. About thirty-six people signed up.

To be clear, I don't treat my networking email list the same way I would my reader list. I'd rather not sell my business contacts on my books, affiliate links, and whatnot. That's impersonal because of the direct relationship I have with them. I merely use the email list to work smarter, not harder.

Then, as time went on and I met new folks through networking, I'd mention to them the monthly meetup. If they wanted to join the monthly meetings, they'd just have to sign up through my link.

Fortunately, I ran the monthly meeting for half a year and had a fair turnout. As with many things in life, it didn't last forever because I had to re-prioritize my time for other work-related stuff. I do remain in contact with those video creators and consider them among my closest friends to this day.

Before you toss all your contacts and network professionals into a list, make sure you can do it on your own without relying on that service. You still need to personalize your communication with each person you know. I don't mind being on an email list or two, but it stops being fun if that's the only time I hear from you. Make your network feel wanted, listened to, and appreciated.

Though I admit I also enjoyed gathering a bunch of my peers in one space so they could meet each other without all the normal fanfare—permission, confirmation, repeat, and meet. By gathering them all in one space, it made it so much easier for me, cut down time, and made it more interactive for everyone involved.

HARNESSING THE POWER OF PODCASTING & VIDEO CONTENT

Another reason I gathered a group of video creators for a monthly mastermind was to work together through collaborations. I'd come up with the idea when I thought about how incredible it would be to have over fifty video creators working on one massive collaboration. Though it never came to fruition, my good buddy, Shanon "S.D." Huston pretty much did that.

Shanon knows the power of video to grow her brand, reach more readers, and connect with other creators. She'd spent a couple years grinding it out on YouTube, finding new author-based YouTube channels, and becoming the consummate networker. After arranging countless co-hosted live streams and meetups with authors, she launched AuthorTube Writing Conference (AWC).

The AWC isn't your typical live virtual event. Where most virtual conference organizers use webinar software and services to obtain and monetize attendees, AWC functioned more like a massive

YouTube collaboration. Shanon worked with dozens of author-based YouTubers—aka authortubers—and arranged three tracks of learning on various times over three days.

It was all free. Yep, Shanon is my kind of crazy. She knew that all these channels working together could create something truly special for their current subscribers and a host of new viewers. After each presentation, the speaker would rattle off the options for viewers to go to next, and then ended their broadcast.

Because of my participation in the first year, I got to meet and work with new authors who were working on YouTube, just like me. It was instant relatability for me, and since Shanon meticulously selected the speakers, panels, and moderators, I knew whoever was involved in the show would be worth connecting with beyond the event.

It's common knowledge by now that over 90% of online traffic comes from video consumption. Couple that with the climb in popularity of video- and audio-based podcasting and you've got a recipe for reaching an all-new audience while making some pretty sweet friends.

You have two entry points into the world of podcasting and video:

1. As a creator
2. As a guest

Obviously, the least amount of work happens at the guest level. You still need to prepare yourself for potential questions while looking your best. As mentioned previously, you'll need to have a few tools in place to make you look presentable. Let's get a bit more granular now.

LIGHTING

For any video guest spots, use ample light to illuminate your face. Natural sunlight is great, but if you're lacking that, you can always use whatever you have in your house—a lamp, a shop light, LEDs, and more.

Position the light source in front of you and slightly to one side. If you have an additional light, place it on the opposite side, and a little farther out. Last, put only a touch of light behind you so you provide contrast between yourself and the background.

It will take some work and tweaking, but once you get it dialed in, you can use that setup repeatedly. Should you find your lights are creating an unusual wash of various shades of white, consider ordering a set of LEDs you can get for about $10 to $30 from any online retailer. Look for a product that allows you to control the brightness and temperature—whether through automated settings or colored gel covers.

CAMERA

You truly need nothing earth-shattering for a camera, but test all the options you have for what looks the best and is the most reliable. Built-in webcams on laptops or computers, mobile devices, and DSLR cameras can work for your needs.

Center yourself on the camera and position it so the lens is a few inches above your eyes and about two to three feet away from your face. Avoid leaving too much room above your head in the shot because it is distracting and puts the spotlight on anything but you. Always be mindful of your positioning. Slouching in a chair and being lazy in your delivery doesn't look attractive. Sit up straight and try to keep eye contact on the camera as much as you can.

Viewers will connect with you when you show them the whites of your eyes. It sounds strange, but how often do you feel invested or trust someone if they're looking away from you? It also breathes a certain air of confidence when you can be present and attentive.

Before you do a guest appearance or interview, ensure your camera can stream for upwards of thirty to sixty minutes or more. I've had a camera or two fail during an interview or live broadcast. It's embarrassing, but it happens. Save yourself the heartache and perform a stress test on your chosen camera before an interview.

MICROPHONE

Most viewers and friends can look past lousy camera quality, but if they can't hear you well or the sound is poor, they're probably going to tune you out. Much like the camera, test it out first by having a friend do a video chat with you. They can give you feedback on how it sounds and if you need a different microphone.

Most onboard mics—whether on laptop, computer, or mobile—are sufficient, but again, don't leave that to chance. Test them. I've found most webcams with the onboard mic are pretty lousy. Those mics pick up a lot of ambient noise and wash out the sound of the person speaking. Not to mention, if you're recording for a podcast, the guest's sound will be messy, making production for the host that much harder.

Do your hosts a huge favor—use a decent quality mic.

If you plan to invest in anything—lighting, a camera, or a microphone—start with audio. You'll find a variety of inexpensive USB microphones to suit any budget. Blue microphones have a ton of great budget options that come with the stand and cord, so it's as simple as plug and play. You'll want to plan on spending anywhere from $15 to $150 for a decent starter mic.

HEADPHONES OR EARBUDS

Though technology has improved a lot over the past decade, there is still room for growth and improvement. Sadly, from time to time, you'll notice an echo during an interview. That's because a guest or host is listening to the other person through a speaker. Zoom and podcasting production companies like Riverside FM come with an echo cancelation feature, but that tool isn't 100% effective. Echoes derail a conversation quick!

Just do everyone a favor—wear a set of headphones or earbuds when you're chatting with another person on video. It eliminates the potential issue of echoes and feedback.

DIRECT INTERNET

Whenever possible, wire directly into the internet so you get the best possible bandwidth. WiFi is unreliable, often creating issues with video buffering or audio latency. It might not have given you problems before, but it very well can happen the time you're trying to make the best possible first impression.

You can still use WiFi if it's your only option. Just make sure you fully disclose that with your host.

BECOMING A CREATOR

I'm rather biased about video content creation and podcasts since I run two channels on YouTube, one of them being a podcast. If you've got even an inkling of a desire to try your hand at content creation outside of your books, then use all the previous advice I gave for guests.

Get good lighting, a decent camera, a suitable microphone and one last thing—video editing software. My go-to program is Camtasia, but that comes at a rather high premium. I recommend looking into the free alternative DaVinci Resolve. There is an endless supply of tutorials for DaVinci Resolve on YouTube, so you aren't empty-handed. Maybe one of these days I'll take a few days out of my schedule to learn this program, but for now, Camtasia suits my needs.

You can get away with shooting a live video or just recording a video and uploading the raw, unedited file. However, you're probably going to have limited results.

Refer to some of my previous advice about creators to follow for more details about producing video content. Podcasts are literally the same thing but without video. I use a free software program called Audacity to record my audio tracks. At the same time, I broadcast on YouTube, so viewers get the actual footage of me recording the audio tracks. Again, you can access a ton of free tutorials for Audacity on YouTube or online forums.

CHAPTER 7
OVERCOMING NETWORKING CHALLENGES

Though I've shared some of my personal challenges in networking, that's only a sample of the issues I've had over the years, even dating back to when I was an activities director in senior living communities.

Networking, in a way, is a lot like dating in that you're going to run into some extraordinary people and some not-so-nice individuals, too. In a lot of instances, you may not have very much chemistry with them. Does that make either of you bad? No. It comes down to unique personalities that may or may not mesh well. Don't take it personally when someone doesn't want to connect with you.

Always assume the best in people when they're communicating with you. A short answer doesn't mean they don't want to talk. It could be bad timing or a conversation that doesn't merit much response from them.

I once co-hosted a live stream where we had several guest experts pop on for ten to twenty minutes. My co-host and I took turns keeping the conversation upbeat and moving. I met one guest for the first time on-air. The discussion spilled over into multiple ways of monetizing a brand, so naturally, our guest mentioned affiliate marketing.

To keep all the viewers in the know, I asked our guest what affiliate marketing was. As a host, it's always best to put the spotlight on your guest, to make them shine by answering what others may not know. Our guest went from energetic and enthusiastic to stern and terse. Unfortunately, she interpreted the question as a challenge, resulting in a few minutes of awkwardness.

Since we were streaming continuously, I never had the chance to catch up with this guest. One year later, we ran into each other at a conference. We connected on a far more positive note with no issues between us. Again, never see the worst in people. Sometimes, you're just catching them on a bad day, or they might have misread you.

DEALING WITH REJECTION & SETBACKS

You would've thought I learned my lesson with the Joe and Raul story, right? Nope, I made an even worse blunder, but this time it wasn't something within my control.

I'm always on the lookout for great video creators on YouTube in the writing and publishing space. No one should measure the value of the content based on the size of the audience. I've found some truly gifted and wonderfully talented video creators with under 1,000 subscribers.

I've discovered some fantastic channels over the years and have watched them grow as more people saw the same thing that I have. I can provide an entire guide of all the folks I follow on YouTube. It's that deep. Sadly, some great creators gave up after a while or moved on to brighter pastures. Video content creation isn't for everyone. The level of passion you have for videos should be similar to your passion for books.

A while ago, I ran into a channel that had great production, including excellent camera quality, as well as superb video editing. The host was upbeat, even chipper, in his delivery, making his videos about publishing all the more fun. I gobbled up every one of his videos and even commented on a few.

Before long, he reached out to me to get connected and to talk about potential collaborations. For the sake of this story, we'll say his name is Don. From the get-go, Don and I hit it off big time. Even though we only booked half-hour sessions to video chat, we ended up going for double, if not triple, that much time.

I appreciated how intelligent and well-connected he was in the industry. That's why it shocked me to see he had a channel with a meager following. It was a matter of time before this gentleman would see his breakthrough, but it was going to be a long, hard road, as I'd learned. Every content creator travels their own path, so it could be easier or harder for him than it was for me. No one can truly predict a breakthrough on YouTube.

For all the great things I found in him as a network peer, I noticed a few questionable behaviors that brought my guard up. First, the man claimed time and again about having wealthy celebrities and experts as collaborators. When I searched the people he talked about, I never found a shred of evidence he was involved with them in any way. Next, he reached out to another network peer and close friend, then name-dropped me even though I never gave permission.

Yeah, remember the whole permission-based system? It works when you want to introduce yourself to someone new while leaning on a shared business associate. It might go something like this:

> *Hey, New Person I Don't Know, I'm a huge fan of your work and would love to chat. I know Dale L. Roberts, a mutual friend of ours...*

I never like to send any of my peers to fend for themselves like that. Sure, I give myself more work in the initial connection, but at least both parties will know my direct involvement serves as an endorsement.

The other way? No way! So many things can go wrong, not to mention anyone could say they know me or are friends with me. Not many of my peers and contacts are going to require proof, because my reputation precedes me. That's why this was the first real red flag with Don.

I overlooked that one little faux pas, because even I make mistakes like that because of my impulsive nature (see the Joe and Raul story). We continued on like nothing was wrong and even planned to do an interview exchange. I'd interview him and he'd interview me for us to share on our respective channels. The other friend he contacted had gotten roped in for an interview, too.

As the date approached, Don changed plans. He wanted to make the interviews a premium event where viewers had to pay for access. That may not seem like much of a change, but it was enough for me to stop everything.

Don and I got on a video chat to discuss the misunderstanding.

CHAPTER 7: OVERCOMING NETWORKING CHALLENGES

"Hey, buddy," I said, "I had absolutely no intention of monetizing these videos. It's better if we make them public so more people can watch and share your channel while getting to know you. And I'd prefer not putting a paywall over content I'd normally share for free on my channel."

Briefly flustered, Don wasn't one to back down. He went into a hard sales pitch about how it would be so nice, and everyone would benefit from the premium event.

In a polite yet delicate way, I pointed out the disparaging difference in audience sizes. I brought most of the viewers, while he only accounted for a fraction of that. His email list was nothing notable either, so I had to break it to him. He stood everything to gain and nothing to lose while leveraging the audience I'd taken years to build. The man took it well, and we continued our conversation as if no confrontation ever happened.

The next day, I checked my LinkedIn DMs to see he'd had an extreme change of heart. Don was furious and spared no feelings when expressing his absolute disdain and disgust for me. I wasn't mad at first, just shocked and disappointed. For minutes after reading this diatribe, I replied with a simple:

Are you okay? Am I missing something?

This was no joke. He was very serious and the only way for him to back down was if I agreed to do this paid interview series. All this after he called me names, cursed, and read me the riot act. Once I realized he was irrational and not the man I assumed him to be, I cut ties.

Even after I blocked him, he sent a barrage of hateful emails threatening me and my friend. Oh, yeah, news travels fast. Apparently, if you treat someone poorly, they're probably going to share it with their friends and network.

After that bizarre interaction, Don disappeared for good, leaving his YouTube channel abandoned.

We can extract several lessons from this story based solely on Don, but I wanted to share more about how I handled it the best way I could—with professionalism, poise, and tact. Once I realized he wasn't returning any respect, I knew he had to go.

I can't generate enough scenarios for you to fully prepare for networking setbacks and rejections. The only way to handle it is the best you can. Will you get it right every time? Possibly not. I know I'm not perfect, but I certainly do my best, as you should, too.

When I've been in over my head, I reach out to a peer for advice. Sometimes it helps to have an ear to bend and someone to help you understand how to do better business or how you can improve. Should the occasion arise, take a step away and seek help from a friend. It's done a lot to preserve my sanity while helping me maintain grace under fire.

MANAGING TIME & BALANCING NETWORKING WITH WRITING

While I'd love to give you the secret formula to managing your time effectively to get everything done in your business—including writing, reading, editing, publishing, marketing, promoting, and more—it's next to impossible to cover it all. The reality is it's tough to juggle all those things, and this is coming from a guy who's married with no kids and two cats. Beyond my family responsibilities, I write content and produce videos. That's it.

For anyone with kids, a day job, or any additional commitments outside of an author brand, it's going to take a lot of planning, flexibility, and patience to find something closely resembling balance.

Start with identifying your priorities in life. Don't hold back. Just write them all down in no special order. I don't care if you think it's a minor role; if you have to do or be present for something consistently, that's a priority.

Now, think about what's most important to you in the long term. Place those priorities at the top of the list. Drop the less important items toward the bottom. Eventually, you should have a list of priorities; how you organize your days, weeks, months, and years should honor this list.

When you feel you're not getting results from what you're doing for your author brand, analyze your daily tasks and action items. Pinpoint whether you're taking actions that benefit your priorities or are you just doing busywork.

Every self-help guru says it best:

> *We all have twenty-four hours in a day. It's what we do with them that counts.*

First and foremost, always prioritize your family. If you are single with no responsibilities, then you're good to go. Next, if you're a writer, then write. And do a *lot* of it! If that's what you want to be, then you need to do the work. It's up to you how you organize the rest, but put some emphasis on networking consistently. It could be once a day—social media makes it easy—or once per week.

Again, that's fifty-two points of contact if you make one per week for a year. It's easy because I'm not insisting you cold prospect for new contacts. You could revisit old connections or join any number of the groups, organizations, and masterminds.

A little can go a long way. If you spend one hour per week networking, that can be sufficient. Spend any more time than that? All the better! I'll admit to you it's hardly a part-time job and the hours fluctuate from one week to the next based on my workload. If I'm overloaded or have approaching deadlines, I'm going to deprioritize networking.

When my workload lightens a bit, I do a little more outreach.

Truthfully, I've been networking for so long that it's second nature to me. One of my preferred networking activities is introducing folks. It's even better when I can make a virtual introduction through a video chat or in person. I like to introduce two of my current contacts per week, so they can get to know each other and support each other how they see fit.

Prioritize your schedule while ensuring you include networking as a small piece of your author workload. You can even label networking under marketing and promotion, because again, your efforts will make you more visible and build awareness of your brand.

BUILDING RESILIENCE & MAINTAINING MOTIVATION

You'd think after being in this business for a decade and running over some rather rough terrain on my journey that I'd become discouraged. You'd be right because I have experienced soul-crushing discouragement. I've sometimes been outright distraught to the point of wanting to quit and return to my old day job.

After taking a break and coming back to an issue, I have to refocus on why I do all this. No one can ever guarantee that success is going to be easy or that everything you do is going to be fun. While it's upsetting when you suffer setbacks or rejections, remember your reason for getting into this author business. Take some of the bad with the good, because that's what will make you truly appreciate the crowning achievements or the first-time interactions with someone new.

When you build a vast network of business professionals and readers, you'll have all the positive support and love you could need. Don't let the few setbacks and bad apples spoil what you have.

Don't give up, and remember to lean on a friend when you're in need. That's one of the best parts about building your network.

CHAPTER 8
NETWORKING FOR BOOK MARKETING AND PROMOTION

All this networking business is well and good, but at what point can you expect to market and promote your book? After all, you don't want to have more busywork that takes away from building your author brand. It's a valid concern because, until now, I haven't really given you any concrete examples of when to market and promote your book.

The whole art of networking seems to focus on direct and virtual person-to-person contact, so when is it okay to push your book through your network?

It depends on the situation and the connections you've developed with your peers. I could make the argument that you already indirectly humble-bragged about your book when you developed your elevator pitch. When you have the perfectly crafted introduction, you won't ever have to beat anyone up to check out your book. The mere fact you are a published author is enough to draw attention.

Authors are a rare breed despite millions in existence today. Beyond those millions are billions of other folks who quietly yearn to put pen to paper and craft that book they've held in their hearts for years. Personal and professional responsibilities restrict these aspiring authors. Not to mention, they lack the resources and insights published authors already have.

When an aspiring author meets a published author, it's a pretty big deal. I know through first-hand interactions that merely mentioning I've written a book—make that plural—is enough to draw out the usual phrase:

> *How cool! I've always wanted to write a book;*
> *I just haven't had the time.*

Or they mention they don't know how, so they're eager to pick my brain. Being a published author has its perks and is one of the easiest icebreakers to strike up conversation, fit for even the most seasoned wallflowers—including yours truly.

I can attend a networking meetup with high anxiety and stress with zero intent to engage with anyone. Before I know it, someone comes up to me and asks the old question, "What do you do?"

Though I'm reserved at in-person events, it doesn't mean I'm meek. I simply step up to the plate and take my best swing at being the least awkward I can be. That's why I have my elevator pitch committed to memory. Once I give my answer, you'd swear my newfound connection just saw a fireworks display, and typically what follows is a free-flowing conversation about what I write, where my books reside, and how the other person can do it too.

What I won't do is meet someone for the first time, cram a book in their hand, and then ask them to market and promote it for me. You can imagine just how abrupt and abrasive that can be.

Leveraging your network for book marketing isn't a tightrope walk. You simply have to rely on intuition to sense when the time is right. If you're the type of person who doesn't feel worthy of asking or is afraid of rejection, it's perfectly natural to avoid asking altogether.

Here are few indicators that you're ready to market and promote your book through your network:

1. You're on a first name basis with your peer.
2. You've talked with your peer at least on three or more occasions for longer than a half hour at a time.
3. The other person asked you about it.

You'll notice the latter one seems like a given, but some authors miss the boat because they're too busy thinking about what to say, how to say it, and when is a good time to ask for help.

When you've built a solid rapport with someone in your network, chances are likely they're going to ask you what you're up to and how they can help. That's why it's always a good idea to lead with goodwill in your network.

When you can be of service to your network, they'll be of service to you when you're in need. That's not to say you should constantly badger your network for favors. Be selective about how and when you ask for help.

For instance, if you're rapidly releasing a book every two to four weeks, then it might not be a good idea to beat up your contacts that frequently. Choose one good promotion, then go from there. As mentioned previously, timing makes all the difference, so if I'm in a conversation where my contact offers help, then I will not wait until my next big promotional campaign. I'll just get them queued up with what I'm currently working on because they asked.

Selling to your network is not enough. It's what my old publishing mentor Jason Bracht would say is "stackin' pennies." Yeah, you'll get a few sales through your network, but you're missing the bigger picture if you're simply selling to just one person. Instead, leverage their reach, audience, and resources to make the most of a promotional campaign.

That's why instead of trying to sell to your network, consider other more impactful marketing and promotional strategies that'll drive your book sales through the roof and build awareness of your author brand.

COLLABORATING WITH INFLUENCERS & BLOGGERS

Straight-up, one of the most nerve-wracking times I have had in this business was asking one of my heroes and indirect mentors, Julie Broad, to write a foreword for my book, *The Amazon Self Publisher*. She'd already picked up and read the series and gave me high praise for the work. Naturally, when I wrapped up compiling this collection into one tome, I thought of Julie Broad.

Julie built a massive presence on YouTube before I ever did. I watched all her videos and shared her content with anyone who'd listen. Through a few brief interactions in the comments and then later via email, Julie and I became great friends.

We later collaborated on a few videos, interviews, and even continued sharing each other with our audiences. But I never really have grown out of viewing Julie as my hero and the social media influencer she's come to be.

I knew that having Julie's name associated with my book would lend a lot of credibility. She put years into growing her brand with her company Book Launchers and has helped countless authors fulfill their lifelong dream of becoming an author.

In my head, I thought she would say "no" or request some ludicrous upfront fee or imbalanced revenue share.

As much as I thought I knew her, she proved every bit of my monkey mind wrong. Julie was happy to accommodate and to this day, she requests copies of that book to distribute to her new clients.

Influencers and bloggers are still a rather untapped market for promoting books and seeking collaborative opportunities. Some folks view "influencer" as a dirty word, only reserved for the elite Kardashian-level celebrities or over-the-top MrBeast-like content creators. The fact is you're missing the ocean of other influencers who may not have a million followers but 100-engaged and dedicated fans.

One of the huge reasons I almost never turn down an interview is that regardless of the size of the host's audience, they're a new audience for me to be in front of. Not to mention the other knock-on effects through building an asset with another creator.

Finding the right influencer or blogger comes down to research. Only you are going to know who best fits your needs and has the ideal audience you want to shoot for. Remember, a bigger audience doesn't always mean it's better. For instance, you might land an interview on the Joe Rogan Experience, but that doesn't mean Joe's audience will resonate with your books or your niche.

I'd rather find a podcaster, influencer, or blogger who has a tiny following with the exact audience I need to reach than a mega-influencer who has a general interest in my wares.

CHAPTER 8: NETWORKING FOR BOOK MARKETING AND PROMOTION

How you find the right people to work with is as simple as:

1. Googling it.
2. Asking around.

This is where your network will serve you best. Ask your peers what podcasts, blogs, websites, and social media influencers would fit best for your content. Even more important, find out if they've worked with authors before, reviewed books, or even offer sponsored post options—if you have the budget for it.

Speaking of paid spots for your books, tread with caution. Not all paid opportunities lead to an instant return on investment. Think of sponsored spots as a good way to build brand awareness, and less about how many book sales will happen right away from your efforts. There are exceptions to the rule, but the most effective influencer marketing comes through a genuine interest in a product, service, or, in your case, a book.

Over the past year, the viral short-form video platform TikTok has seen a rise in the hashtag #booktok. Quite a few authors have benefitted big time from this organic movement, including the breakout success of Colleen Hoover.

Now, I don't have any data or inside intel if Colleen or her publisher paid for those spots, but every video I found pushing her books didn't have a sponsorship disclosure, indicating the post is 100% legit and unpaid.

Your network is going to give you suggestions and recommendations on who might work for you and where it's best to share your books. Referrals from within your network can be priceless, especially since you spend less time banging out search after search through Google.

The conversation can be as simple as emailing your contact or arranging for a brief video chat. Any time I'm looking to get the best results, I will lean in favor of a video chat.

As an example:

Hey, Jason,

I'm getting ready to launch my next book, Sweet Werebear Romance, *and I'm looking to make a big splash on launch week. Who do you know on social media that would be a fit for marketing and promoting my book? I'm looking for influencers on any level, regardless of the size of their following.*

Also, if you know of any websites or blogs that fit, that'd be helpful too. Thanks so much!

Feel free to use that as swipe copy but customize it in your voice. It doesn't need to be put together through deep manipulative Jedi mind tricks to be effective. Just ask. When the time is right, your peer will return the favor and request your referrals or recommendations to assist them in their business.

Just a friendly reminder, referrals are the best way to do business because it removes the ambiguity and comes with a stamp of approval from someone you trust.

The best part about asking for a referral, like in the previous example, is that's an indirect way of marketing and promoting your book. Then, it's less in your face and a lot more subtle. I've found many times that's effective in driving book sales that I hadn't even accounted for.

SECURING ENDORSEMENTS & BOOK REVIEWS

Once you've built a robust network of business professionals, gotten to know them on a deep level, and can trust them with most aspects of your business, it's time to see if they'll go the extra mile.

In the indie publishing world, I've heard the term blurb used in reference to the book description, but it also is the label used when an outside source provides a brief review of your book.

When someone within your network wants to buy and read your book, ask them for their honest feedback. Be prepared because you may not get the answer you were expecting. Fortunately, besides my first book, I've always received positive and encouraging feedback. Quite a few times, my peers have left reviews in various places.

The biggest issue with getting a review from someone you know is the inherent bias related to your direct connection. Places like Amazon frown upon biased reviews and will even delete them if they detect a connection. Rather than encouraging your network peers to leave a review on an online retailer, ask them to post it on their site, social media, or share it through their email newsletter.

Ask for permission to use all or parts of that review on your book cover, product page, website, or social media. Anyone with an audience or influence online can lend a ton of credibility to your book, especially if they're a perceived expert.

For example, if you wrote a book about dieting and nutrition, getting a blurb from a dietician, family doctor, or any medical practitioner can go a long way in signaling the authenticity of your work. I'm an avid horror reader who has seen several authors in my preferred genre with blurbs from famous names like Stephen King or Dean

Koontz. Having these two prolific horror writers provide a stamp of approval is enough to make even the most discerning reader stop and give that book a shot.

You cannot have too many blurbs, so if you have someone within your network willing to read and review your work, do it! Just make sure you get their permission in writing to share parts or all of their review, so no toes get stepped on.

Getting blurbs or reviews is a never-ending task you can pursue for the rest of your life and still not get enough. Don't be afraid to ask when the occasion arises.

MAXIMIZING NETWORKING OPPORTUNITIES DURING BOOK LAUNCHES

Launching your book is the publishing equivalent of delivering a baby. It's a glorious day and everyone should share in the joy. Anyone who crosses your path should feel your excitement and enthusiasm. A great network of business pros will be just as excited as you are and be ready to help wherever possible.

I save my biggest favors or requests from my network for book launches. While I don't publish as frequently as I used to, it's certainly at a pace that won't burn out my network when I ask for help in promoting a book launch.

The first thing you should do before a book launch is to make an extensive list of everyone you know. Your list can include everyone in your network, friends, and family. Once you have the list, organize and prioritize time to outreach with each person.

Focus on what will give you the most visibility in the weeks leading up to and following your book launch date. Should you not have a pre-order page, I recommend sending early traffic to your email list so they will be notified when the book is live and where to get it.

Prioritize video interviews and collaborations, as well as any relevant podcasts. The key is to schedule each appearance on separate days so you get more consistent exposure over the long run.

For anyone who doesn't have a social media following, email list, or significant reach, have that person be an ambassador for you. Sharing your book with their modest following—whether online or in person—is enough to help spread the word. Take no one for granted on a book launch.

If you're going to lean on your network or anyone else for help, at least provide them with a promotional copy, whether digital or print. I am a bit more frugal these days and only offer print if that's the only way the person reads a book. Otherwise, I have StoryOrigin host my ebook and send my folks to download their copy through them.

All your networking efforts will pay off when you launch your book. If you're lacking results or not selling as many books as you'd expect, take a step back and analyze how you can better approach the next launch and leverage your network. If your book flops, it's not the fault of your network. That's on you, so you have to determine what you can do better, which includes expanding your network and increasing your reach for future launch campaigns.

CONCLUSION: NETWORKING FOR LONG-TERM SUCCESS

I'll admit I'd actually forgotten altogether about introducing my two friends, Kathleen Sweeney and M.K. Williams. The thought never crossed my mind that I'd get something out of the connection. Quite simply, I made the introduction because they are two really outstanding people who I knew would get along.

I'm not over here keeping score, waiting for Kathleen or M.K. to return the favor. I merely think about it from a different yet slightly selfish standpoint. The connection between the two has built a bigger circle of friends. If we ever meet in person, I will have two friends who are already familiar with each other, so our conversations will flow smoothly and we will have a great time.

I realized in the initial phone call discussing this book with Kathleen that I'd made the connection between the two. The funny part was they've gotten along marvelously since then without any of my intervention. That's not just good; it's great.

Thankfully, I've kept in semi-close contact with both women. From time to time, M.K. will pop up in my DMs on Discord just to check in on me. What a gem! Side note: You need a few people like M.K. and Kathleen in your network. They're priceless.

SUSTAINING RELATIONSHIPS WITH INDUSTRY PROFESSIONALS

I truly can't think of just how many folks in my business network keep in regular contact with me. I'm rather fortunate. In return, I drop a brief note, send over a question, or check in with them, too. A little goes a long way, so I never take for granted the impact of a single-sentence email for staying in touch.

You don't need to hound them every week. Make it organic as possible and less of a job. That's why I view networking less like an action item in my business and more so about meeting and staying in contact with some pretty exceptional people.

From time to time, you will find someone you especially gel well with. Don't be afraid to lean into that relationship. The year before last, I had the privilege of meeting Nick Thacker—prolific author and VP of Author Success at Draft2Digital. I love me some Nick and he has been generous not only with his time but his insights and experience. Getting to know Nick has been one of my greatest blessings in this business and in life.

Had I been uninterested in networking, I would've never gotten to know Nick the way I have. Between learning about better voice dictation, becoming a prolific writer, or providing levity when I needed it most, Nick is my go-to dude.

You'll find many business professionals that you absolutely adore. Just don't let your existing relationships overshadow other folks who could lock arms with you and race with you to the finish.

A large part of your networking should include following up—and not just with the Nicks in your lifeline. Consider meeting them where they are most comfortable, whether by social media DMs, emails, or in comments. You'll know what works best with them based on their response. When in doubt about where to contact them, just ask.

CONTINUING PROFESSIONAL DEVELOPMENT & LEARNING

While I'm confident you've got all the tools and insights you need to be effective in setting up your network, I understand there are some ambiguities and questions left unanswered. Nothing trumps learning better than doing. You just have to get out there and do it.

Look into local meetups, conferences, networking events, and online social mixers. When you can't find one you like or want, make one and invite all your peers. If you're feeling really squirrelly, you can always have them bring a guest and have that guest bring more guests. There is no limit!

I learned some of my most valuable lessons in networking by going to countless in-person networking meetups in Phoenix, Arizona, with Rod Bailey. While I'm sure he'd be flattered that I recommend following him for all his networking appearances, I think it might get weird if too many people trail him.

What I recommend instead is digging into your network to find the veteran business mind—that person who smells like smoke because they've been through fire. You'll know they're a pro when you see them approach a random person at a party with drink in hand and strike up a conversation like they've known this stranger for years.

Will you be able to act the same way as Rod Bailey would? Well, that comes with time, practice, and a little self-awareness. If you're anything like me when you arrive at an event—find the water cooler and hang out by it—then you probably will not meet very many folks. It's hard to chat with the random, strange guy in the corner looking like a lost puppy by the water cooler.

I start conversations by finding someone who isn't engaged with another person or group. Then, I simply approach them with a basic question that'll at least start us talking. Some of my conversation starters aren't the greatest, but it's enough to break my crippling anxiety and loosen me up enough to keep going.

Worst-case scenario, find a group of folks in a circle and just join them. Eventually, you'll be able to interject or add value to the conversation.

As for continuing education, you could look into classes on networking, but they're all going to say the same thing I have, just differently and with alternative strategies.

Nothing beats education like experience. So, get out there and meet someone, whether or not you're good at it.

EXPANDING YOUR NETWORK AS YOUR WRITING CAREER DEVELOPS

With time and practice, you too will build a deep network of business professionals. As your writing career matures, so will the relationships within your network. Don't simply rest on having six or seven great contacts. Expand your network and you'll expand your horizons.

You don't have to obsess over networking so it consumes your every waking moment. Think of it as an ancillary part of your business. As long as you put in a little effort over the long run, you'll see it pay off in dividends through greater reach, more book sales, and an increased readership.

Remember, you are only one contact away from something big. Whether that's a traditional publishing deal, movie option, foreign translation rights, or more, there's always one contact who can make the biggest impact on your career.

That's where the unrelenting power of a network shines the best for authors. One contact at a time, you'll grow your author brand into something so much more massive than you could have ever done simply on your own.

Now, get out there and meet somebody new and grow your network today!

A SMALL ASK...

Now that you've finished reading, I'd love to hear your thoughts. Did you find any tips particularly valuable? Is there something you feel could be improved or added? Your honest review on the platform where you picked up the book will help others decide if it's right for them and guide future updates.

Your feedback is crucial for refining the book and supporting other indie authors. Thank you for your time!

Or post a review here: DaleLinks.com/ReviewNetworking.

GET MY BESTSELLER BOOK LAUNCH CHECKLIST ABSOLUTELY FREE!

Want to launch your book to bestseller status on Amazon? Sign up for my email newsletter today and get my **Bestseller Book Launch Checklist** for FREE! This step-by-step plan will help you make your book a hit.

But that's not all! When you subscribe, you'll also get my email newsletter packed with the latest self-publishing news and tips. Get all you need to know in just one or two emails per week.

Subscribe now and grab your free checklist at
DaleLinks.com/Checklist

ABOUT THE AUTHOR

Dale L. Roberts is an award-winning author and video content creator. After publishing over fifty titles and becoming an international bestselling author on Amazon multiple times across various regions, Dale started his YouTube channel, Self-Publishing with Dale. After eight years of producing high-quality content about self-publishing, Dale has cemented his position as the go-to authority in the indie-author community.

Dale currently lives with his wife, Kelli, and two rescue cats in Columbus, Ohio.

Relevant links:

- My Books—DaleLinks.com/Bookshelf
- Website—SelfPublishingWithDale.com
- YouTube—YouTube.com/SelfPublishingWithDale
- YouTube Podcast—YouTube.com/@SelfPubWithDale
- Discord—DaleLinks.com/Discord
- Twitter—Twitter.com/SelfPubWithDale
- Facebook - Facebook.com/SelfPubWithDale
- Instagram—Instagram.com/SelfPubWithDale

SPECIAL THANKS

I'm forever grateful to Rod Bailey for instilling in me the value of networking. Reflecting on the four plus years of working under him, I rarely viewed him as a boss. He was a leader in every sense. Those dozens of network meetings really paid off, and I'm so glad Rod brought me along for the ride every time.

Also, I can't say enough kind words about my network of business professionals and friends. This includes Jeanne De Vita, Kathleen Sweeney, M.K. Williams, Dr. Rod Bailey, Shannon Vlogs, Kevin Tumlinson, Jonny Andrews, Brian Meeks, Jake Crist, Sylvia Hubbard, Dan Currier, Shanon "S.D." Huston, Hannah and Jay Jacobson, Julie Broad, Keith Wheeler, Evan Gow at StoryOrigin, Jason Bracht, Nick Thacker, Mark Leslie Lefebvre, Dave Chesson, Jim Azevedo and the Draft2Digital team, Marco and Natasha Moutinho, the Dibbly Team, the KDP Team, Self Pub with Andy, Bill Latoria, Thomas A. Bradley, Mark Brownless, Mojo Siedlak, Matty Dalrymple, April Cox, Justin Moore, Nuria Corbi, Steven Seril, Jason Jones, Chelsea Bennett and the Lulu Press team, and the list goes on. If I didn't mention your name, it's not a reflection of your value, more so of my memory. I'm forever grateful for all you do and for you being part of my life and business. You are the best!

RESOURCES

- Fiverr – DaleLinks.com/List
- Dibbly Create – DaleLinks.com/DibblyCreate
- Shut Up & Write – ShutUpWrite.com
- StoryOrigin - DaleLinks.com/Storyorigin
- Authortube Writing Conference - AuthortubeWritingConference.com
- Camtasia – SelfPublishingWithDale.com/Camtasia
- DaVinci Resolve – BlackMagicDesign.com/products/davinciresolve
- Audacity - AudacityTeam.org

www.ingramcontent.com/pod-product-compliance
Lightning Source LLC
Chambersburg PA
CBHW071720020426
42333CB00017B/2340